BAMBOO CONTEMPORARY
Green Houses Around the Globe

William Richards

————

PRINCETON ARCHITECTURAL PRESS · NEW YORK

For Ava

Published by
Princeton Architectural Press
70 West 36th Street
New York, NY 10018
www.papress.com

© 2022 William Richards
All rights reserved.
Printed and bound in China
25 24 23 22   4 3 2 1   First edition

ISBN 978-1-61689-900-4

No part of this book may be used or reproduced in any manner without
written permission from the publisher, except in the context of reviews.

Every reasonable attempt has been made to identify owners of copyright.
Errors or omissions will be corrected in subsequent editions.

Editor: Kristen Hewitt
Designers: Paul Wagner, Paula Baver

Library of Congress Control Number: 2021950390

BAMBOO CONTEMPORARY

CONTENTS

Bamboo's Continuum Is Architecture's Future

In design circles, bamboo has been heralded as the material of the future—a pliable solution for architects seeking sustainable methods and materials. But for many architects and builders along the equatorial band, bamboo's past is just as rich. It's both new and nothing new at the same time, and this book addresses that duality in profiling contemporary houses around the world that have utilized bamboo to advance the design vision. In some cases, bamboo, itself, is the vision.

The grass we call bamboo is considered a quaint curiosity compared to the steel, masonry, concrete, glass, wood, and polycarbonate that dominate the design and building industries. But, bamboo captures the imagination in a way that other materials don't. You see bamboo in escapist encomiums to indifference like Anthony Bourdain's *Gone Bamboo* (1997), about two expat assassins in the Caribbean. You see it in Paul Gauguin's paintings of Martinque and later, more famously, of Tahiti. Bamboo is a uniquely renewable plant that has long been employed as structural, decorative, nourishing, and useful—facts known by preindustrial cultures from Asia and India to the Americas, between the Tropic of Cancer and the Tropic of Capricorn. It also tran-

scends notional categories of high and low culture. Take the flute as an example. Bamboo flutes are indigenous to two dozen countries, and include the *atenteben* of Ghana, the *bansuri* of Nepal, and the Andean *siku*, a kind of pan flute that requires the player to apply their embouchure along a row of connected culms, or hollow stems. Many productions of Mozart's enigmatic 1791 opera *The Magic Flute* often feature, unsurprisingly, a Chinese *dongdi* or *dizi*, and the Library of Congress holds a 1950 first edition of *La petite méthode des faiseurs et joueurs de pipeaux de bambou* (or The little method for makers and players of bamboo pipes), by the composer Camille Evieux-Lamberet, whose little method remains unchallenged to this day.

Eastern Woodland tribes in North America have used bamboo for centuries to carve flutes, weave baskets, fashion weapons, and craft jewelry, and although the United States claims only one native species of bamboo, *Arundinaria*, its growing region stretches from the mid-Atlantic to the Florida Panhandle. Florida's once abundant thickets of bamboo, known as canebrakes and the natural habitat for the state's now-endangered panthers, have been diminished by development and agriculture.

During the Federal period and after, American furniture makers from Maine to Maryland used bamboo to create Windsor chairs, which were often stained or painted to achieve a uniform patina. In 1798, Thomas Jefferson took delivery of a padded Windsor bench with six turned bamboo legs ("a stick sopha and mattras"), made by Lawrence Allwine of Philadelphia, and used it to prop up his legs while reading and writing. Today, the Monticello gift shop sells a similar prop for your reading chair featuring a "gold-leafed, bamboo-turned steel frame with thick padded seat in a stunning marbled print."

In this vein, bamboo's role in the domestic sphere for the last fifty years has mostly been decorative, driven by interior designers and decorators eager to mask the anonymity and sterility of modern architecture. If you read Terence Conran's *House Book* (1974), *Kitchen Book* (1977), or *Bed and Bath Book* (1978), one gets the distinct impression that it's a cover-up job. Homeowners are given detailed instructions on how to aggressively decorate as an act of personal expression as much as an act of erasure. In The *Apartment Book* (1979), Ali MacGraw, one of the celebrity owners profiled (along with Jill Clayburgh and Richard Dreyfuss), explained her decorating philosophy: "I love natural canvas coverings, real treasures on the walls, a few antiques, old pine." Pith aside, against the backdrop of drywall and unrelenting orthogonals, the point of these books is that modernism could be sufficiently warmed up as to be livable with enough patterns, textures, tiles, and macrame hanging planters. But lurking in photos of MacGraw's home, behind a lot of decorative items in various shades of brown, are several bamboo elements, like tortoise roll shades and a wall grid of pots and pans in the kitchen composed of whole bamboo culms, which offered, above all, a way to cover a lot of white walls.

Since then, design magazines have trumpeted bamboo's return every decade as a "natural" decorative element and, on occasion, faux bamboo as the basis of a "fresh look" around the home. From placemats to Thonet-style chairs and window blinds, the allure of bamboo is about its versatile appearance, from refined to rustic, and its warmth, in a range of hues mostly on a scale from tan to chestnut. In the last twenty years, bamboo has come to reflect a shifting consumer sphere—as polyester and plastic once did—and a product that incorporates bamboo always seems to be within arm's reach. My local Target sells 288 products that are wholly or partially derived from it. The neck of the soap dispenser in my bathroom is made of it. The small cutting board in my kitchen is bamboo. The shelves in my infant daughter's room are bamboo. Next door, in my preteen daughter's room, she is knitting a scarf (for her sister) using bamboo knitting needles. The coaster on my desk is bamboo. The runner, ribs, and handle on my umbrella are bamboo, and, since I've had it for nearly twenty years, I can say that my bamboo-handled umbrella has proven far more durable than the flimsy metal pieces that have sent other, lesser umbrellas into early retirement.

Bamboo has also come to reflect corporate endorsements of renewable materials, sustainability, and supply-chain ethics. Corporate responsibility often connotes both social and environmental responsibility, and bamboo (and bambooish) products are on the front lines of both base consumerism and protective regulations. In 2010, the US Federal Trade Commission (FTC) chided nearly eighty retailers (after suing four the year before) for selling products labeled as bamboo fiber and touting bamboo's antimicrobial properties. The fabrics in question might have started life as bamboo fibers, but chemical transubstantiation turned them to rayon, as blood to wine. The ruse didn't end there. In 2015, the FTC collected penalties totaling $1.3 million from Bed Bath & Beyond, Nordstrom, JCPenney, and Backcountry.com for continuing to advertise bamboo products that were anything but. Even Shakespeare was drawn into the scrum. Announcing the penalties and terms, the FTC intoned, "Maybe 'a rose by any other name would smell as sweet,' but deceptively describing rayon clothing as bamboo isn't so sweet—and violates the FTC's Textile Rules." Since then, companies have become more transparent in their labeling, and the FTC has left the Bard alone.

Today, market analysts project 5 percent annual growth in a nearly $70 billion industry over the next five years in bamboo products of all kinds, both refined and unrefined. Bamboos (as grasses) and rattans (as palms) are uniquely situated to ameliorate several environmental concerns as they can absorb more than a third more carbon dioxide and produce a third more oxygen than most trees. Bamboo species are renewable and resilient, and although they may prefer tropical climates, some can grow farther afield. I see bamboo growing in yards all over my neighborhood in Washington, DC, which is technically on the outer edge of the subtropical zone. Most homeowners here utilize bamboo patches as privacy screens and property dividers. Some will lament that they can't get rid of their bamboo patches, owing to the aggressive root system, so they simply learn to live with them. Nevertheless, their wild patches add a lovely dimension to a fairly predictable area with brick row houses, center hall Colonials, and squat bungalows.

"Many people consider bamboo a rampant, obnoxious, ruining, and uncontrollable plant that's nearly impossible to remove once established in a garden, and they fail to see all the uses bamboo has," says Luc Boeraeve, the president of the American Bamboo Society, who cites its strength, resilience, and adaptability to different needs like whole culms for scaffolding, half-culms for bahareque mud construction, plywood for cabinetry, or woven mats for flooring. "It is," he notes, "a natural product, it is renewable, it grows well in locations less favorable for most agricultural crops, it stores crops, and it provides employment in remote areas."

Still, says Boeraeve, "it is very hard to convince people once they are prejudiced against bamboo." In 2012, at the height of bamboo's newfound product celebrity, the American Bamboo Society issued a statement about invasiveness and control in response to what its members felt was a critical mass of misinformation in the media and on the lips of frustrated homeowners with bamboo patches. Their concerns were entirely founded. Garden magazines, shelter magazines, DIY blogs for yard warriors, and even well-meaning but ill-informed nursery employees at the local garden centers have all decried bamboo's invasiveness. Even the US Park Service has called it, on occasion, an invasive species and has employed a number of tactics (including goats) to eradicate it from its properties.

The truth is that bamboo is a perennial with a rhizomatous growth habit, which is to say its roots are thick and spread out horizontally underground, and it can grow quickly in a short period of time. So-called "running bamboo" species grow aggressively, while "clumping bamboo" species grow more slowly. Some people find bamboo, with tensile strength likened to steel, difficult to manipulate in their yards or eradicate. Where some see limitations, however, Boeraeve sees potential beyond its strength as a building material and its flexibility to resist earthquakes: "Bamboo can provide food, heating and cooking material, and shade. Bamboo can remediate degraded landscapes, and it's

a natural habitat for birds, pandas, and endangered species like mountain gorillas."

But will bamboo ever succeed as a natural habitat for us? Boeraeve, as well as several architects I've talked to, points to immature or nonexistent supply chains and a lack of standard and uniform quantities of construction-grade bamboo for a middle-class mass-housing market. For designer-driven, custom projects, like the ones featured in this book, bamboo is available to architects and builders who often have to string together multiple growers and suppliers to get the culms they need in the quantities they need.

So how can architects close the gap? They actually have a lot of choices, even within the limited market of bamboo-derived products. Bamboo laminates for flooring and bamboo-fiber wall systems, paired with natural insulators, like wool, show a lot of promise for the mass-housing market, particularly in places like China, Brazil, and the United States. At the theory level, bamboo has gained purchase with a cadre of architects interested in public interest design and sustainable urbanism. In 2016, Pritzker Prize–winning architect Alejandro Aravena advocated for bamboo in his plenary address at Habitat III, the UN Conference on Housing and Sustainable Urban Development. At the case-study level, architects and designers working on groundbreaking projects in the last decade have used bamboo at different scales to great effect. Boston-based MASS Design Group's GHESKIO Tuberculosis Hospital in Port-au-Prince, Haiti, completed in 2015, features bamboo privacy screens covered in bougainvillea vines as a way to help patients feel like individuals rather than outbreak statistics. Washington, DC–based KUBE Architecture's 2015 competition entry for a Peace Corps monument is a plaza-sized, woven bamboo structure that, in one Mobius-strip-like twist, acts as a bridge and a shaded alcove. Shigeru Ban's 2016 green-bamboo-clad emergency-relief structures for Ecuador utilize his signature cardboard tubes as the structure and split culms in a herringbone pattern that form strong windbreakers and effective sunshades. When used to its greatest potential, bamboo allows us to literally grow our own homes. We're not there yet, but perhaps these projects will stoke some interest in bamboo as a persuasive choice from the spoon to the city. This book, then, is a stake in the ground for bamboo, around which one hopes architects are inspired to push for its adoption and improve its market and distribution worldwide.

THE PROJECTS

AURA HOUSE
BALI, INDONESIA

Ibuku, 2018

The Aura House is one of several structures at Green Village, a private community of custom homes near the Green School, an alternative school started by jewelry designers and bamboo champions Cynthia and John Hardy in 2006. Green Village's nineteen homes and the Green School complement each other as test sites and laboratories. The arrangement conjures the Dessau campus of the Bauhaus, where art and craft created a seamless connection between classrooms and dormitories. It also conjures Arcosanti in Arizona, where, since the early 1970s, living and working have coexisted as a grand experiment that's both aesthetic and moral.

But Green Village is something a little different. Its villas take up more than 61,000 square feet of luxury living space, which is billed, notably, as representing "luxury bamboo." This is not an oxymoron at all for Ibuku and its founder and creative director Elora Hardy but the synthesis of two worlds, the highbrow and the handicraft. At the Aura House, different textures, both tactile and chromatic, are created throughout the interior with woven bamboo, while the structure is entirely blond in color.

"What makes Aura special among those at Green Village," says lead architect Rita Santoso, "is rather than trying to blend in [with] nature, the Aura House wants to stand out." The site for the 328-square-foot project, says Santoso, includes black sugar palm trees, which she describes as offering a "Jurassic, wild-nature vibe." To create that vibe, Santoso's team specified and purchased more than 32,000 feet of Petung bamboo (*Dendrocalamus asper*)—which is native to Bali, Java, and Flores and grows in small patches—from hundreds of local farmers. After it was harvested and transported, the culms were treated with a boron solution to suppress the glucose inside, which would make it unappetizing to the local fauna.

This synthesis of highbrow and handicraft has roots in art nouveau—from over a century ago and more than 7,600 miles away—that, visually, the Aura House evokes. Art nouveau's appeal to the haute bourgeoisie of nineteenth-century Brussels and Paris was partly aesthetic: industrial materials like iron could be manipulated into impossibly delicate and organic forms by hand. It was also partly moral: even after the industrial revolution transformed production and, in turn, art, actual craftsmanship in fin de siècle Belgium and France was still a virtue worth protecting. Hector Guimard's cast-iron vines and buds set in concrete that still welcome Paris Métro riders are the most public and perhaps notable symbols of art nouveau's ubiquity. Less well known is the fact that Guimard also completed dozens of private homes throughout France, as did Victor Horta in Belgium. Notably, Horta used bent iron, glass, and wood for his own house and studio in Brussels to mimic natural forms and create an interior world caught between the urban and the villatic.

"How we feel about design does overlap significantly with art nouveau," says Elora Hardy. "Natural forms, a love of light, and a sensation of space, often with a goal to uplift and inspire. We also seek to blur the lines between the arts and daily life and to seek cohesive unity with the structure by seeing the furniture and detailing as part of the building sculpture." Indeed, the sitting area and small eating area are defined by bamboo chairs and tables, the gentle curves and mottled tones of which seem to have grown right out of the floors and walls. The bedroom is defined by a bamboo platform bed as striking as it is seamlessly integrated into the ceiling, the culms of which create the undercanopy of a water lily.

What Ibuku's designers have been able to do at the Aura House is evocative of Horta and Guimard and a guidepost for architects working primarily in bamboo today. The Aura House is an evolution in the way art nouveau represented an evolution, but this time, Hardy and her team are able to realize organic forms using organic material grown locally and sustainably harvested. "The material is our guide, and we seek to design for it and respect its strengths and limitations rather than bending or twisting it to our whim."

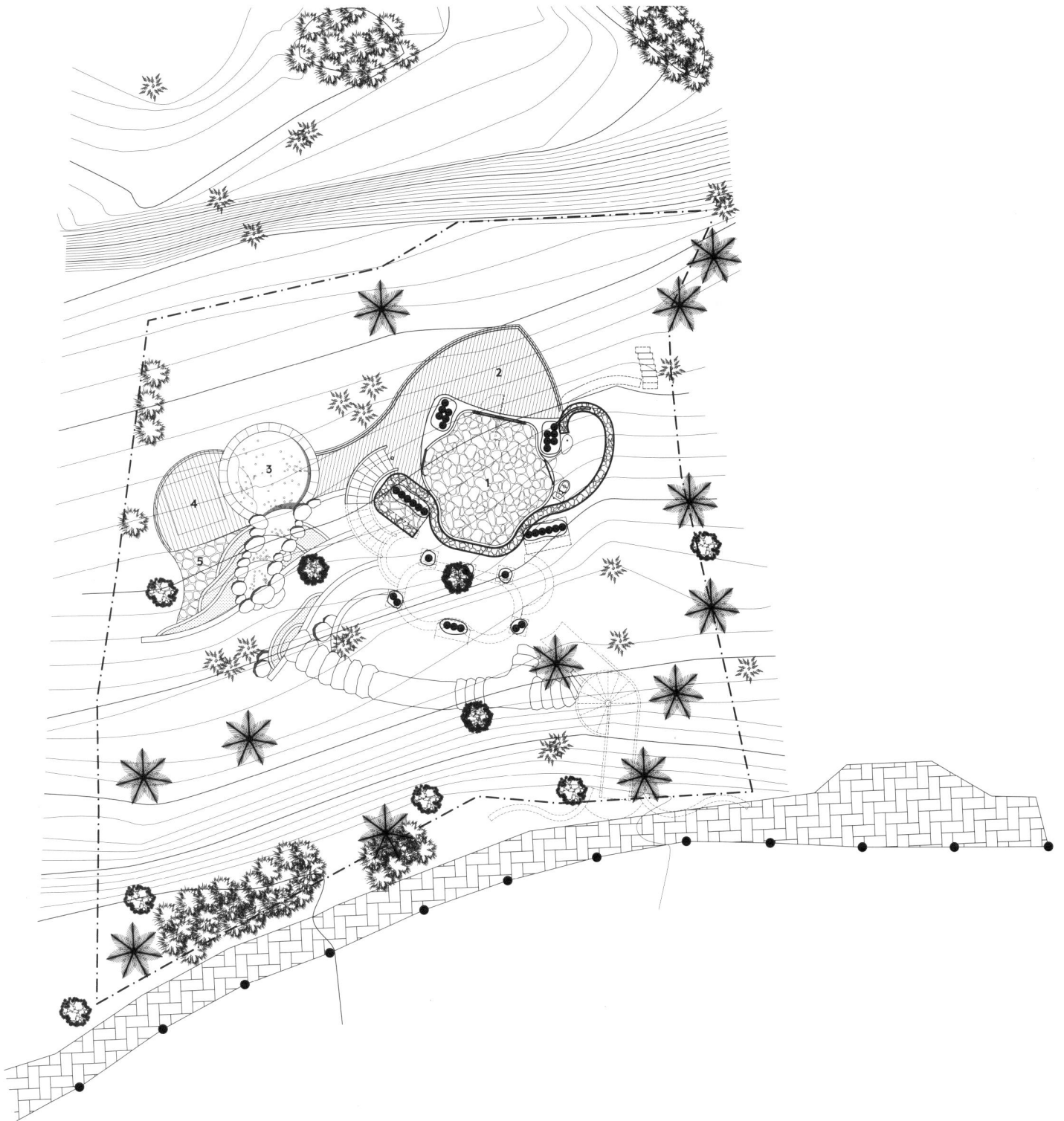

GROUND FLOOR PLAN

⊘ ┌─────────┐
   0   10FT

1. Ground floor bedroom
2. Deck terrace
3. Plunge pool
4. Deck
5. Landing

TANTANGAN VILLA
BALI, INDONESIA

WOM Architecture, 2009

Bali's southwestern coast is known for Tanah Lot, the offshore rocky outcrop that draws tourists day tripping from Denpasar. Its temple, a Hindu pilgrimage site called Pura Tanah Lot, was restored a generation ago after erosion threatened to topple the temple and destroy its cave complex within. Since then, several villas have cropped up less than a mile away on the mainland that participate in the nearly $80 billion (USD) global ecotourism industry, including the 4,600-square-foot rental villa Tantangan Villa, which is relatively isolated and unspoiled by area development.

Modulating the villa's views from within the house—both framing the sea and slicing it like Barnett Newman's "zips" against a color field—are whole bamboo culms evenly spaced and minimally treated. From nearly every vantage point within the house, these culms define the viewsheds and vantages and echo many of the other surfaces in the house—floors, bed frames, riser lips, and bookcases— all done in locally sourced bamboo or bamboo laminate.

In Indonesian, *tantangan* means "challenge," "dare," or "defiance," depending on the context. Valentina Audrito of the firm WOM (Word of Mouth) has noted in interviews that the challenge in designing this villa was about remaining attuned to the environmental context, which the firm achieved by topping each of its pavilions with a green roof. Audrito and Kumbhat describe the pavilions, which surround a large courtyard, as "planter boxes" of a scale that the sculptor Claes Oldenburg would have appreciated.

The project coexists with its scrubby beachside context overlooking the Indian Ocean on Bali's southwest coast, even as its boxy, whitewashed pavilions stand in contrast to the contorted coconut palms, lontar palms, and banyan trees of its site.

Twenty-five miles to the east of WOM's modest villa, Elora and John Hardy have turned an area just beyond the foothills south of Mount Batukaru into Green Village, a bamboo laboratory and spec-home community aimed at changing minds about luxury's responsibility to ecology. The Tantangan Villa is a bit more approachable for the vacationers interested in spending a dozy week beachside, but both efforts at both scales define what's possible in Indonesia and elsewhere not only for the ecotourism industry but also design and construction generally.

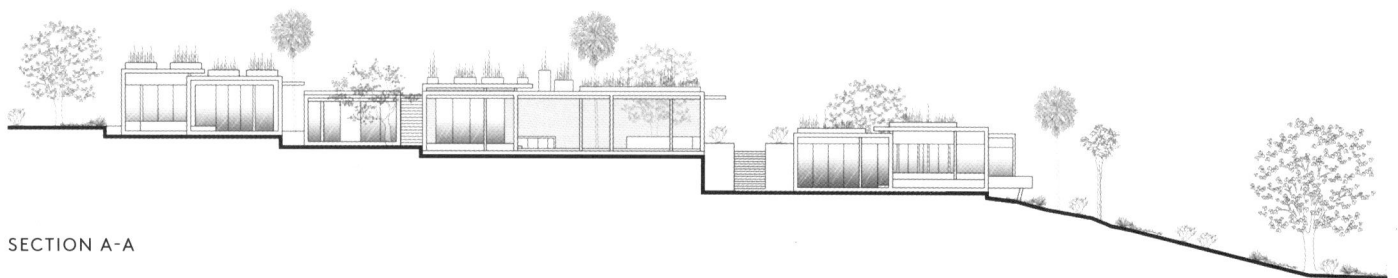

SECTION A-A

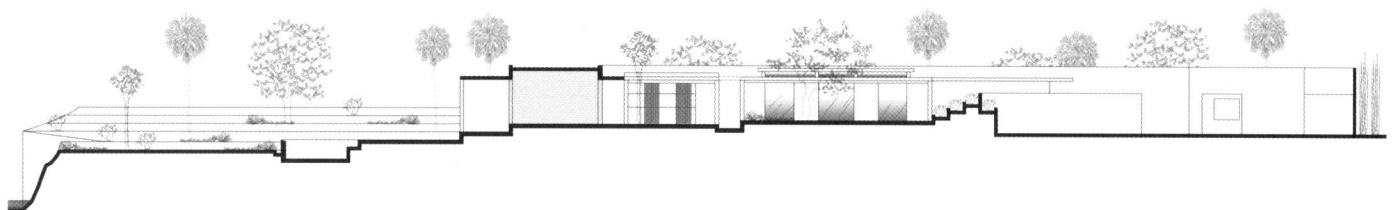

SECTION B-B

B-B

A-A

8

4

5 6

7

9

11 10

3

12

2

13

1

FLOOR PLAN

1. Entrance
2. Carport
3. Temple bedroom
4. Master bedroom
5. Living room
6. TV room
7. Seaview bedroom

8. Swimming pool
9. Kitchen
10. Laundry
11. Office
12. Office bathroom
13. Staff area

0   10 FT

BAMBOO FOREST HOUSE
HUALIEN COUNTY, TAIWAN

ROEWU, 2008

BAMBOO FOREST HOUSE
HUALIEN COUNTY, TAIWAN

ROEWU, 2008

Despite the name Bamboo Forest House, this project in eastern Taiwan does not incorporate bamboo in the structure of the house. Instead, architects Stephen Roe and Chiafang Wu deployed bamboo on the upper floor to create a screen between a busy street and the six-bedroom, single-family home. The bamboo's culms are spaced at regular intervals to create the screen's form and rhythm. But to get the distinctive appearance of an undulating facade, Roe and Wu cut the culms to different lengths and angled them away from the surface of the structure, toward the street.

If you look across the facade at an oblique angle from one corner to another, the screen appears to be solid. In contrast, when you look at the culms frontally, the spaces between them reveal the boxy, conventional shape of the house. In this way, the screen acts as both sieve and second skin. "It is a buffer between the street and the house," says Roe, and "between the public and the domestic spaces." The screen also extends upward to create some privacy for the roof deck, which is "private, yet open to the wind," notes Roe.

From the living spaces within, spare windows frame the bamboo screen beyond, revealing precisely spaced woody culms and their fasteners. Creating visual interest, a paper-thin space between the ends of the culms creates a line of open sky from inside. In addition, the screen offers the practical advantage of having sections that may be replaced over time if needed.

The bamboo screen serves an environmental function, too, for Taiwan's subtropical climate. "It was important for the clients that the house could be allowed to 'breathe' using natural ventilation as much as possible rather than air-conditioning," says Roe. "This was not a radical idea on their part but rather was linked more to traditional ways of living where air-conditioning was not relied on." A house that can "breathe," as Roe puts it, doubled as an opportunity to create a level of privacy on a site in close proximity to other houses on the block and defined by a street that's no wider than twenty-five feet.

But should we consider this house a "bamboo house" at all since the architects have relegated the material to a privacy screen that facilitates passive cooling? For Roe and Wu, the answer is about "formations rather than form," and the fact that bamboo doesn't always suggest a new way of thinking about what a house should look like, but rather, the strong and adaptable material offers opportunities to improve the way a house functions.

There's another layer to the design here, which has to do with the way Roe and Wu designed the Bamboo Forest House with digital software and fabrication tools. The London-based duo sent their three-dimensional digital model of the house, including precise measurements for bamboo-culm lengths, to Taiwan, where fabricators cut and assembled the entire structure to order. "We rather liked the 'low-res' effects of building materials and were looking for ways to marry the craft techniques of construction workers to the digital techniques of representation," says Roe. Bricks, tiles, rods, and culms are small elements that contribute to a finished building, not unlike the zeros and ones that contribute to a digital file that displays on a computer screen—or the "smooth," as he calls it, juxtaposed against the roughness of raw physical materials.

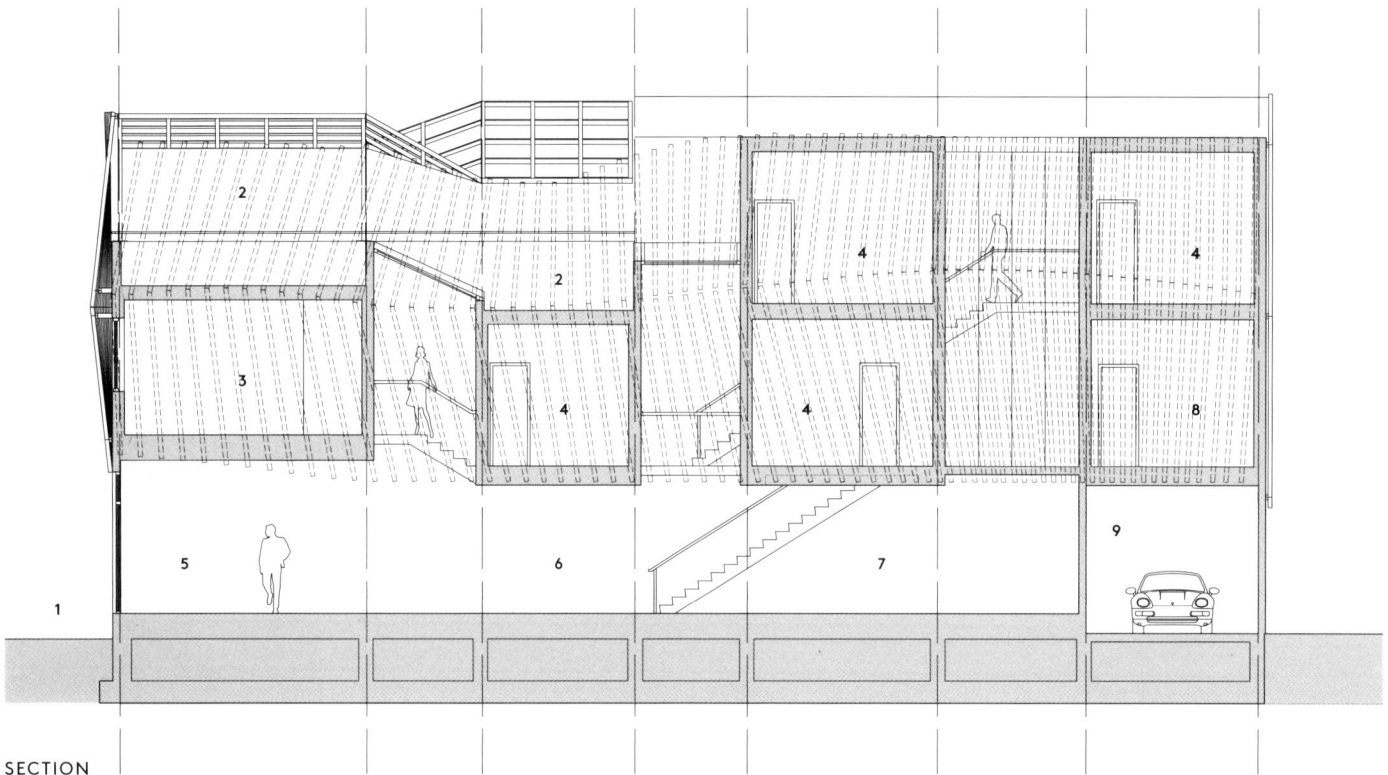

SECTION

1. Garden
2. Roof deck
3. Master bedroom
4. Bedroom
5. Living room
6. Dining room
7. Kitchen
8. Spa
9. Garage

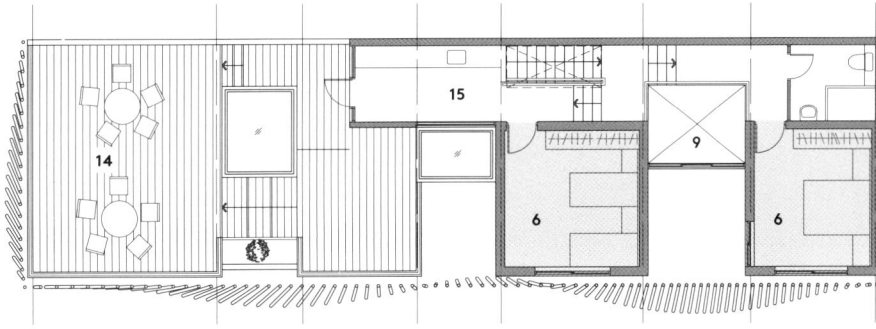

THIRD FLOOR PLAN

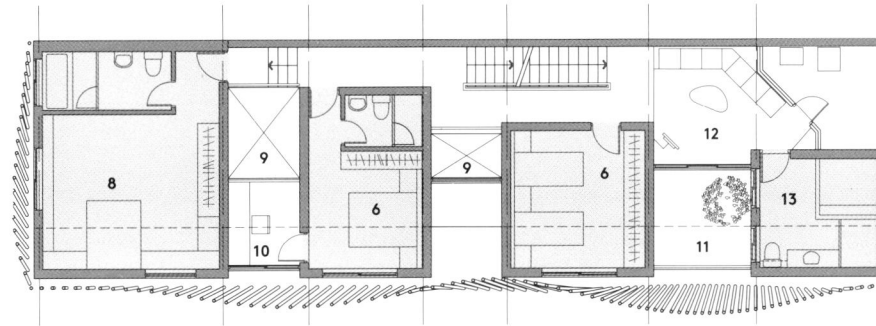

14

15

9

6

6

SECOND FLOOR PLAN

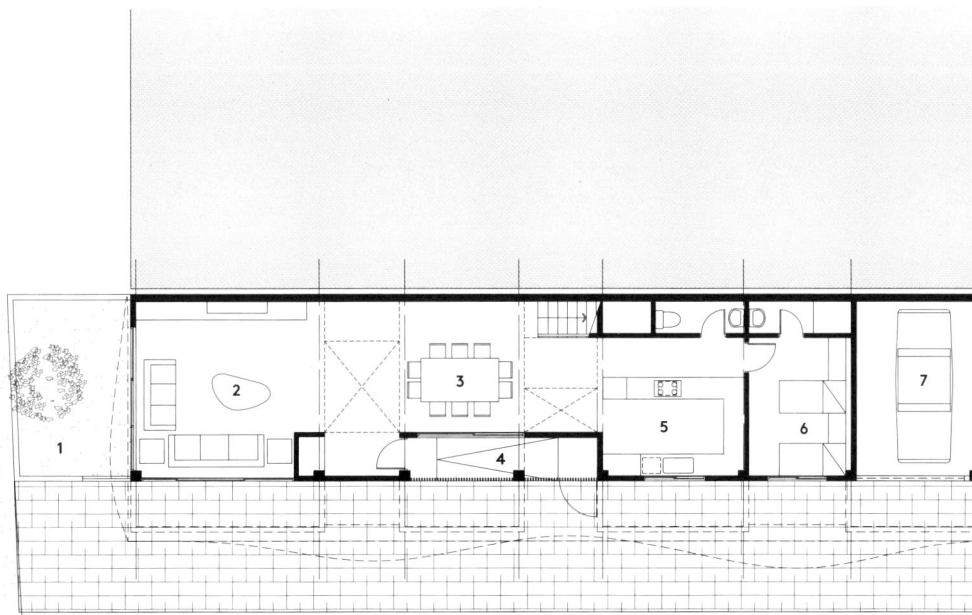

8

9

6

9

6

12

13

10

11

1. Garden
2. Living room
3. Dining room
4. Entrance
5. Kitchen
6. Bedroom
7. Garage
8. Master bedroom
9. Void
10. Study
11. Deck
12. Karaoke lounge
13. Spa
14. Roof deck
15. Bar

GROUND FLOOR PLAN

1

2

3

4

5

6

7

0   10 FT

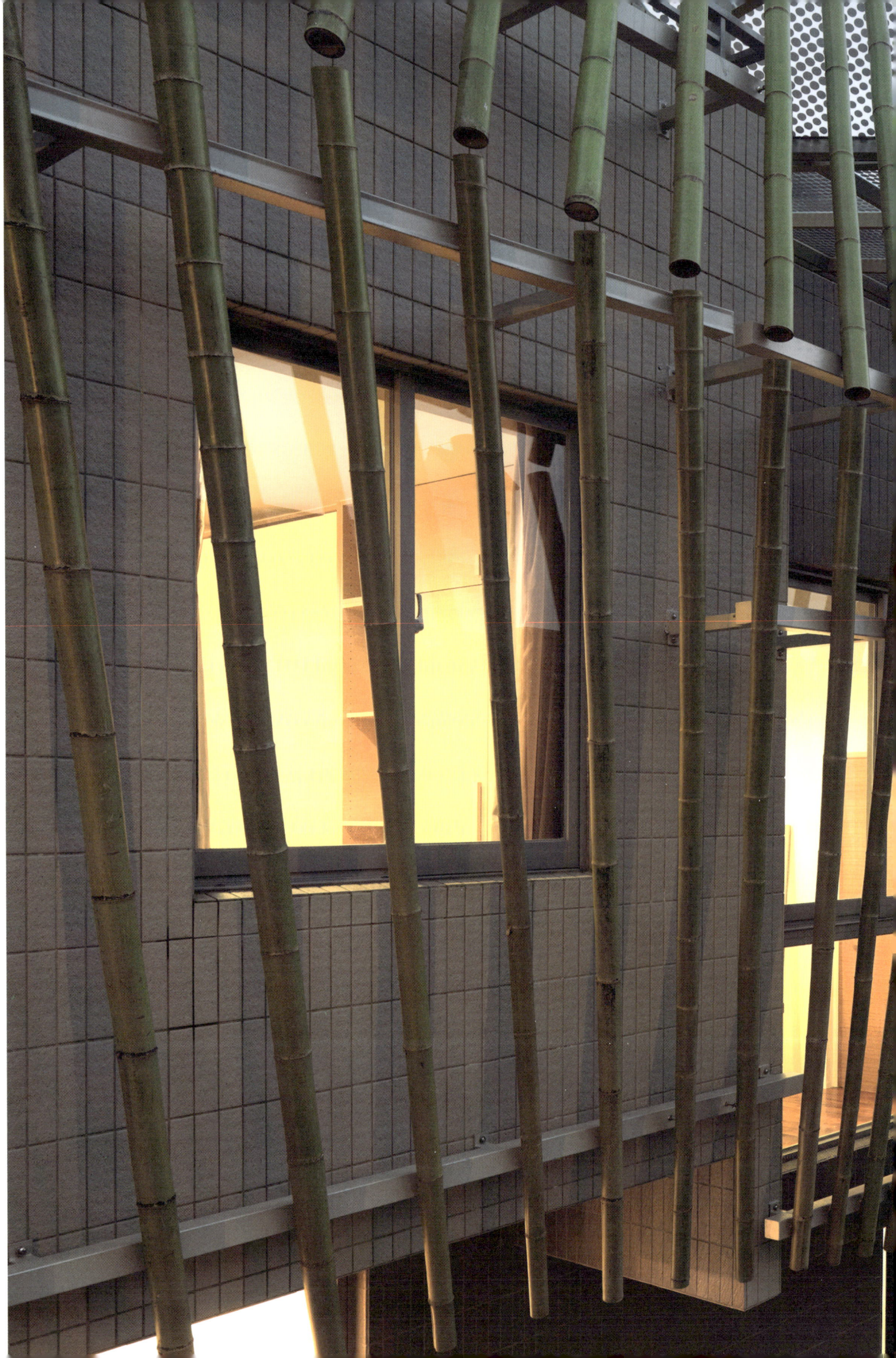

GREAT (BAMBOO) WALL
BEIJING, CHINA

Kengo Kuma and Associates, 2002

The design team at Kengo Kuma and Associates describes this house as a wall, taking their cues from the Great Wall, whose garrisons and rammed-earth fortifications were completed more than twenty-two centuries ago and whose entrance at the Ming Dynasty–era span near Badaling is a little more than a mile away. Since walls can shelter people within (if the walls are big enough), they can technically qualify as houses. But as Kengo Kuma's design team points out, houses can also, indeed, qualify as walls.

The Great (Bamboo) Wall is mostly clad in bamboo over a concrete and steel structure, and its plan is entirely linear. Its ground-floor plan evokes Frank Lloyd Wright's Robie House, which is ship-like in its orientation and arrangement of rooms. This wall-house has long indoor and outdoor passages, which connect a series of rooms. On this particular site, characterized by a sequence of rolling knolls, the house is oriented northeast, toward the Great Wall. In this way, the house-as-wall and the wall-as-house analogies give the project its parti pris. A wall works at the domestic scale as living spaces and on the urban scale as a defensive structure thirteen thousand miles long.

Kuma is one of Japan's most prolific and respected architects and theorists, whose list of projects since the founding of his firm in 1990 number in the hundreds. By the time property developer and architecture patron Zhang Xin invited him to join eleven other architects to design villas for a valley adjacent to the Great Wall in 2000, his decade-old firm was well established and thriving, with several museums and homes under its belt. Kuma's house was completed in 2002, along with those designed by other highly regarded practitioners, such as Shigeru Ban and Antonio Ochoa-Piccardo, among others. The Great (Bamboo) Wall is now a part of an enclave of luxury hotel sites owned by Xin's company SOHO China.

The 5,600-square-foot, six-bedroom house, nestled in a dale overlooking an impossibly beautiful and lush landscape, exhibits the material richness of its bamboo culms inside and out. As interior wall cladding, the culms are spaced tightly to enclose the tearoom overlooking the gorge below, and they are spaced loosely in other parts of the house to define functional spaces while allowing light into the interior. Under direct light, the culms are honey yellow and punctuate the deep brown shadows cast by their ridges, which appear at regular intervals along the vertical axis. Under indirect light, the bamboo culms are a grassy green-yellow, which casts a soft, celadon glaze over the room.

As exterior cladding, the bamboo is blond along some stretches of this wall house and a reddish-brown along others. In some places, the culms are spaced tightly to create a panel that doubles as a sliding light baffle for indoor-outdoor spaces. In other places, smaller panels of culms are arranged in a checker pattern denoting a greater desire for privacy in some of the bedrooms. The tonal richness and play between transparency and opacity Kuma achieves with vertical bamboo culms contrasts with the unremarkable arrangement of rooms—an interior living space defined by material and light. Creating this sort of place is part of what Kuma calls the "anti-object," his design philosophy and a way of privileging the craft and purpose of structural elements over the programs and forms considered to be the bedrock of conventional architecture, residential or not. Can a real object made of steel and glass (and bamboo) exist as an anti-object? An unreal object? Is a building like this home the sum of its joists and joints? Or is it a way of transmitting traditional materials and building practices?

The answers might not matter as much as Kuma's intention to create something useful that meets an elemental need for shelter. "Architecture forms a vital link between people and their surroundings," he wrote in his 2015 book *Small Architecture / Natural Architecture*. "It acts as a gentle buffer between the fragility of human existence and the vast world outside."

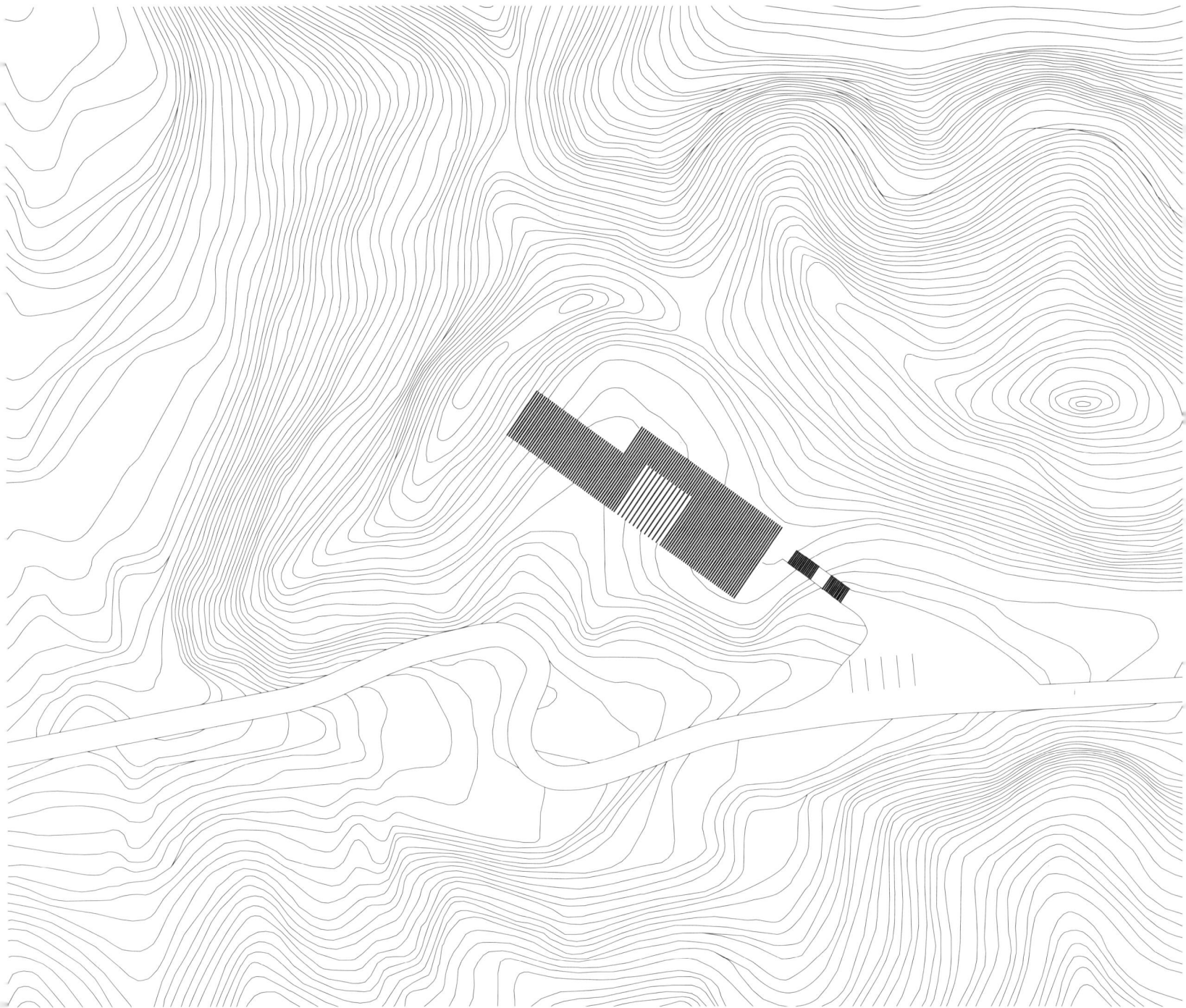

SITE PLAN

GREAT (BAMBOO) WALL

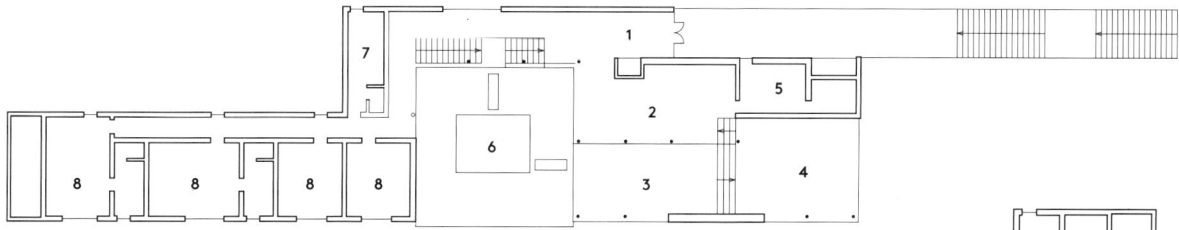

FIRST FLOOR PLAN

1. Entrance
2. Kitchen
3. Dining room
4. Living room
5. Storage
6. Lounge
7. Bathroom
8. Guest room
9. Machine room
10. Staff room

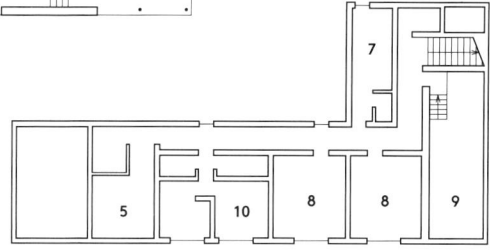

BASEMENT FLOOR PLAN

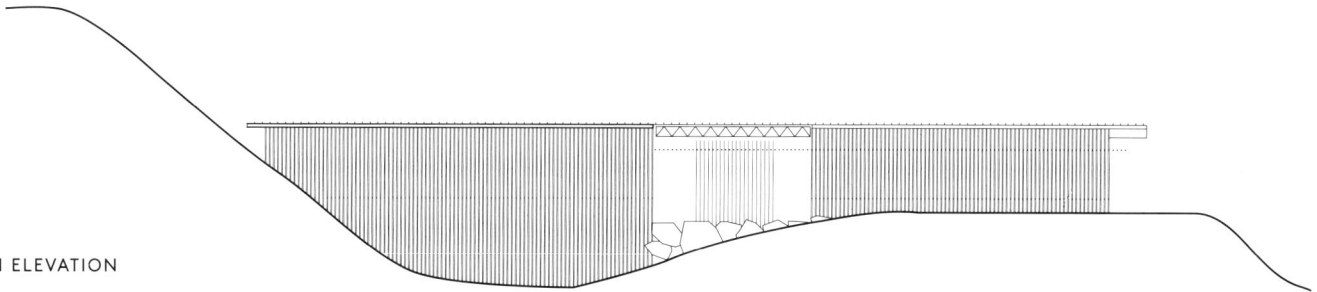

0   10FT

SOUTH ELEVATION

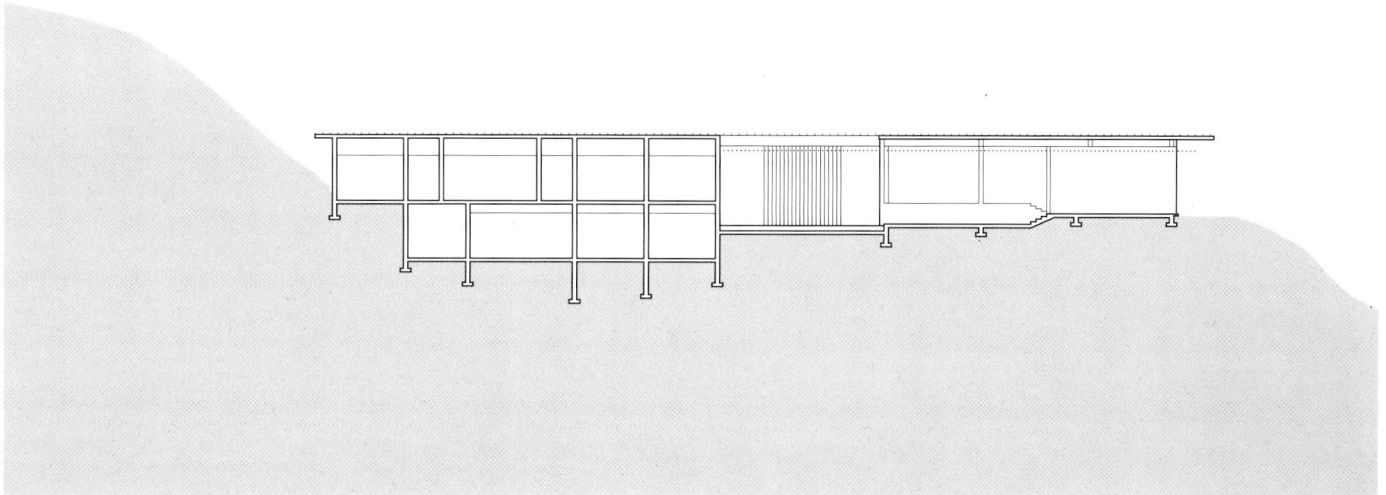

SECTION

RIPARIAN HOUSE
KARJAT, INDIA

Architecture Brio, 2015

The Riparian House frames both a hilltop view adjacent to a river in Karjat, outside of Mumbai, and an interior courtyard centered on a boulder split in two by a stone staircase. Both of these landscapes, one extroverted and one introverted, are fundamental to understanding this house. But they are completely disconnected in space and scale. Scholars cite the Indian yoni-linga as a precedent for the Chinese yin-yang but that idea of symbiotic opposites is perhaps too convenient as a parti for the Riparian House, at just over one thousand square feet.

The truth is that this dependency was a complete accident, says Robert Verrijt, a principal at Architecture Brio, a firm he cofounded with Shefali Balwani in 2006. They intended, at first, to simply design a ramp. "During the design process of the house, we had built a pavilion in the vicinity on a similar hill," says Verrijt. "And through this construction, we learned about the underlying geography of the site and had a hunch about what we would find underneath the layer of soil. So when the idea arrived to build a partly underground house, we were hoping to discover some large boulders that could define a courtyard on the back of the house to allow light and ventilation in the kitchen."

Looking out, the boulder in question is framed by the kitchen eating area's window, ten paces away from where the table meets the window, and it is split by the stone steps leading up to the southeast entrance from the road. Verrijt and Balwani liken this part of the house to Buddhist forest monasteries throughout parts of India and Sri Lanka that negotiate rocky outcrops to incorporate natural elements into their construction. "They give you a sense of enclosure but are also built [as an] invitation to view the landscape surrounding you," says Verrijt. "An experience that is all encompassing and has an essential meditative character."

From the northwestern approach to the site, the Riparian House appears as a series of tiers overlooking the Western Ghats, an escarpment that covers 54,000 square miles and connects six Indian states. The vista from both the master bedroom and kids' bedroom is modulated by generously spaced Burmese bamboo culms, harvested in Karnatka, a state to the south of Mumbai that began subsidizing farmers in 2019 to cultivate bamboo. It's a view that has what can only be called an interscalar quality, which makes the riverbank and trees beyond seem both near and far at the same time. It's a sense of both prospect and refuge, to cite the Frank Lloyd Wright

scholar Grant Hildebrand—a sense of dominion and protection. Indeed, some of the ideas Wright explored in a few of his residential projects, like Kentuck Knob outside of Ohiopyle, Pennsylvania, or Taliesin East in Spring Green, Wisconsin, are evident here outside of Mumbai: being *of* landscape and *in* the landscape at the same time, concentric rings of privacy, and a defined hearth space. That innermost hearth space at the Riparian House is the place where the kitchen, eating area, and doorway to the formal dining room meet: it's a junction for the family to focus on food together and a visual nexus of the home's two opposed landscapes—boulder and river valley, yoni and linga, within and without.

"The purpose of a home in a setting like the Riparian House is to reimagine the relationship of oneself with nature. Apart from framing the landscape, we like to create an experience of place," says Verrijt, who is wary of oversimplifying the oft-heard architectural intentions to "blur the boundaries between inside and outside" or "mimic nature itself." After all, as much as one might try to invite nature in or push living spaces out into the open with patios and pergolas, all architecture is an imposition and, as Verrijt notes, a "confrontation" with nature.

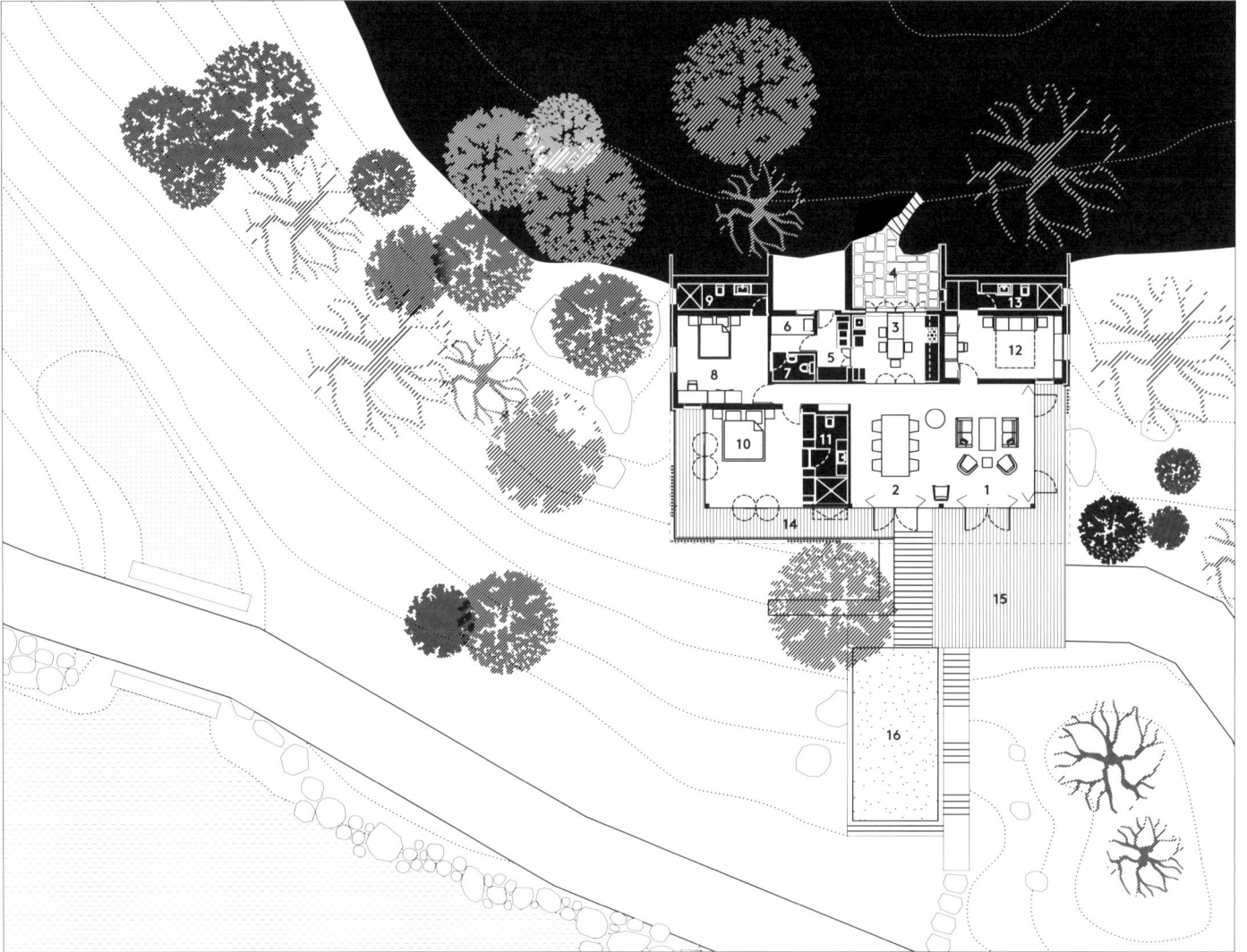

FLOOR & SITE PLAN

1.	Living room	9.	Kids bathroom
2.	Dining room	10.	Master bedroom
3.	Kitchen	11.	Master bathroom
4.	Kitchen courtyard	12.	Guest bedroom
5.	Pantry	13.	Guest bathroom
6.	Staff room	14.	Veranda
7.	Staff bathroom	15.	Deck
8.	Kids room	16.	Pool

SECTION

RIPARIAN HOUSE

BAMBOO HOUSE
BRNO, CZECH REPUBLIC

Atelier Štěpán, 2009

n the interwar period before 1939, Brno, Czech Republic, was fertile ground for modern architects. It was a city where they could find wealthy clients with progressive tastes. There, the Villa Tugendhat, a UNESCO World Heritage Site, stands as the most famous of these homes, designed by Ludwig Mies van der Rohe and Lilly Reich and completed in 1930. Less famous, but essential for anyone interested in the city's functionalist heritage, is the planned suburb Kolonie Nový dům, which includes sixteen International Style jewel boxes completed in the late 1920s, the impossibly narrow Hotel Avion designed by Bohuslav Fuchs and completed in 1928, and the municipal crematorium designed and completed in 1930 by Arnošt Wiesner.

Brno is nothing if not eclectic, however. While glossy travel magazines trumpet its allure as "an undiscovered hotbed of modernism," its architectural history includes traditional Moravian-revival-style buildings, Soviet-era buildings of every stripe, the thirteenth-century Špilberk Castle, and the Cathedral of Saints Peter and Paul, which was built over several centuries. It seems fitting, then, that a project called the Bamboo House by local firm Atelier Štěpán should be built in Brno—as a modest contribution to sustainable building practices today and a nod to modular-design theory from a century ago.

Designed by Marek Štěpán, the 1,400-square-foot Bamboo House is aptly named. Bamboo is everywhere: as flooring, as encasements around beams, as privacy screens along the exterior gallery, and as room dividers within the home. Its applications are not structural, but bamboo is integral to the client's lifestyle. "The house is designed for a family whose members lean toward Eastern philosophy and like natural materials," says Štěpán.

From the outside, the home looks like a progressive, design-forward contribution to the neighborhood. It combines gray concrete with warmer bamboo tones that carry a historical reference to Maison Dom-Ino, a portmanteau combining *domus* and *innovation* for a modular housing concept by the architect Le Corbusier. Štěpán's early design renderings are explicit about the connection. But, as built, the use of bamboo screens along the exterior conceal that reference enough to make it seem to almost subvert not just Le Corbusier's influential prototype but modern architecture too.

On the other hand, perhaps the use of bamboo for a Maison Dom-Ino form is actually appropriate given that Le Corbusier, whose real name was Charles-Édouard Jeanneret, often retreated to his rustic cabin on the Côte d'Azur to paint and write—a cabin that stood in complete opposition to his formal architectural vocabulary and progressive ideals.

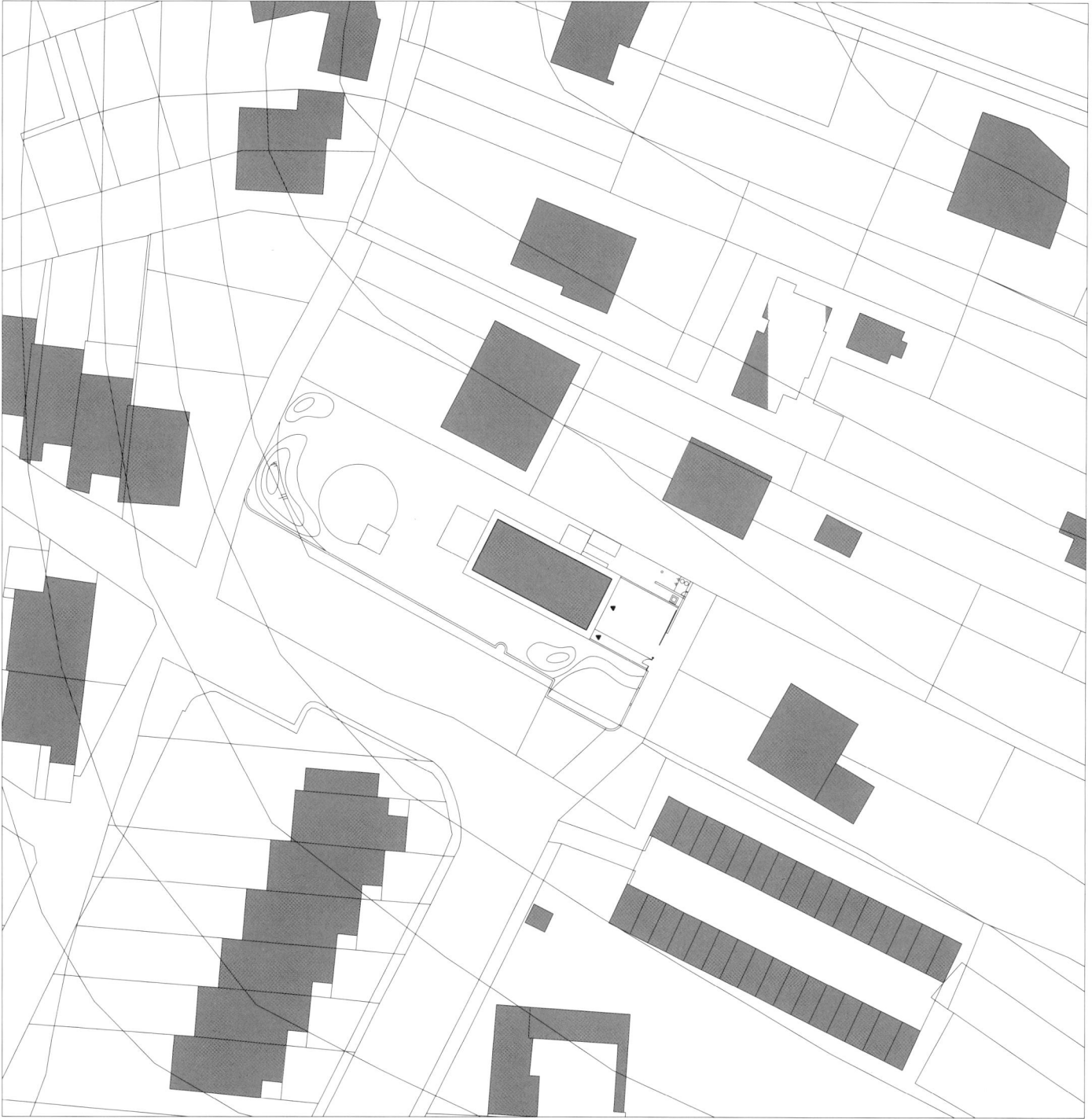

SITE PLAN

0   10 FT

ENEBOLIG SØMME
OSLO, NORWAY

Knut Hjeltnes, 2013

Enebolig Sømme, completed in 2013 by architect Knut Hjeltnes, is a prefabricated single-family home for Christian Sømme, who commissioned it for his family, including four young children. Enebolig Sømme, meaning "detached house," is decidedly modern with its unadorned orthogonal volumes perched on a hillside. But Hjeltnes's work is a much softer addition to both the land and the surrounding area of suburban Oslo, owing to his use of bamboo cladding, which offers a chromatic transition from structure to sky in the same way that the brown shingled rooflines do for the nondescript homes in the area.

The vertical syncopation of culms, precisely spaced like a whale's baleen for the top floor's facade, also offers a visual transition against the scrubby grass below and the sky above. The bamboo's warm tones offset the exposed concrete of the ground-floor walls, but Hjeltnes is counting on it to weather to an ashy gray. Enebolig Sømme's perch offers its homeowners pleasant views of the area, but it's also nakedly visible to an entire neighborhood, as sections of the upper facade's bamboo cladding swing open to let light in (and let the world in). They also close to provide the kind of privacy one might want for the upper-level bedrooms. "We knew that bamboo could be left untreated, turning grayish with time," says Hjeltnes. "The hidden windows on the top floor and the gray, bland look would make it look more like an outbuilding than a regular house from a distance, and more anonymous."

The project's sitework is limited to a concrete slab that extends up to form the bottom half of the house, embedded in a steep hillside. The top floor was assembled off-site and craned into place, then clad in bamboo. No stranger to prefabrication, Hjeltnes also had his acclaimed 2018 weekend house, called Straume for a fjord island in Oslo, craned into place by boat. The site for Enebolig Sømme a few miles away might as well have been a hard-to-reach fjord island tucked behind an established neighborhood. "The difficulties of the site were not so much connected with the fact that it is sloping as the fact that it is very limited, cramped," says Hjeltnes.

Enebolig Sømme is not a hytte for the weekend, but it does stand apart from the workaday homes in its Oslo suburb. "We always hope that our actions will result in some kind of poetic dimension," says Hjeltnes. "The basis for everything we do in the office is listening to the situation, the client, and the place, and to interpret this in a way that is meaningful at this specific moment in both time and place."

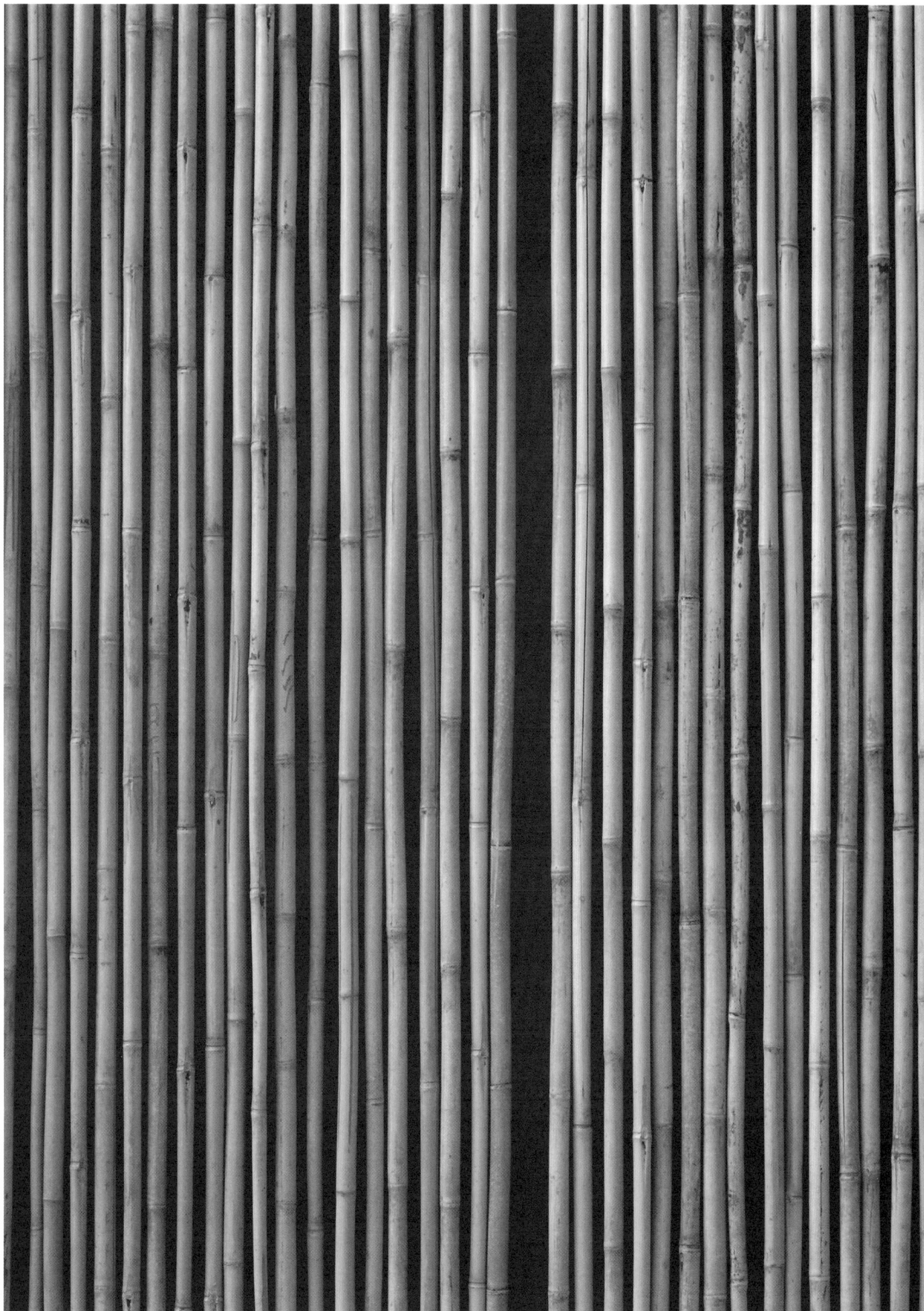

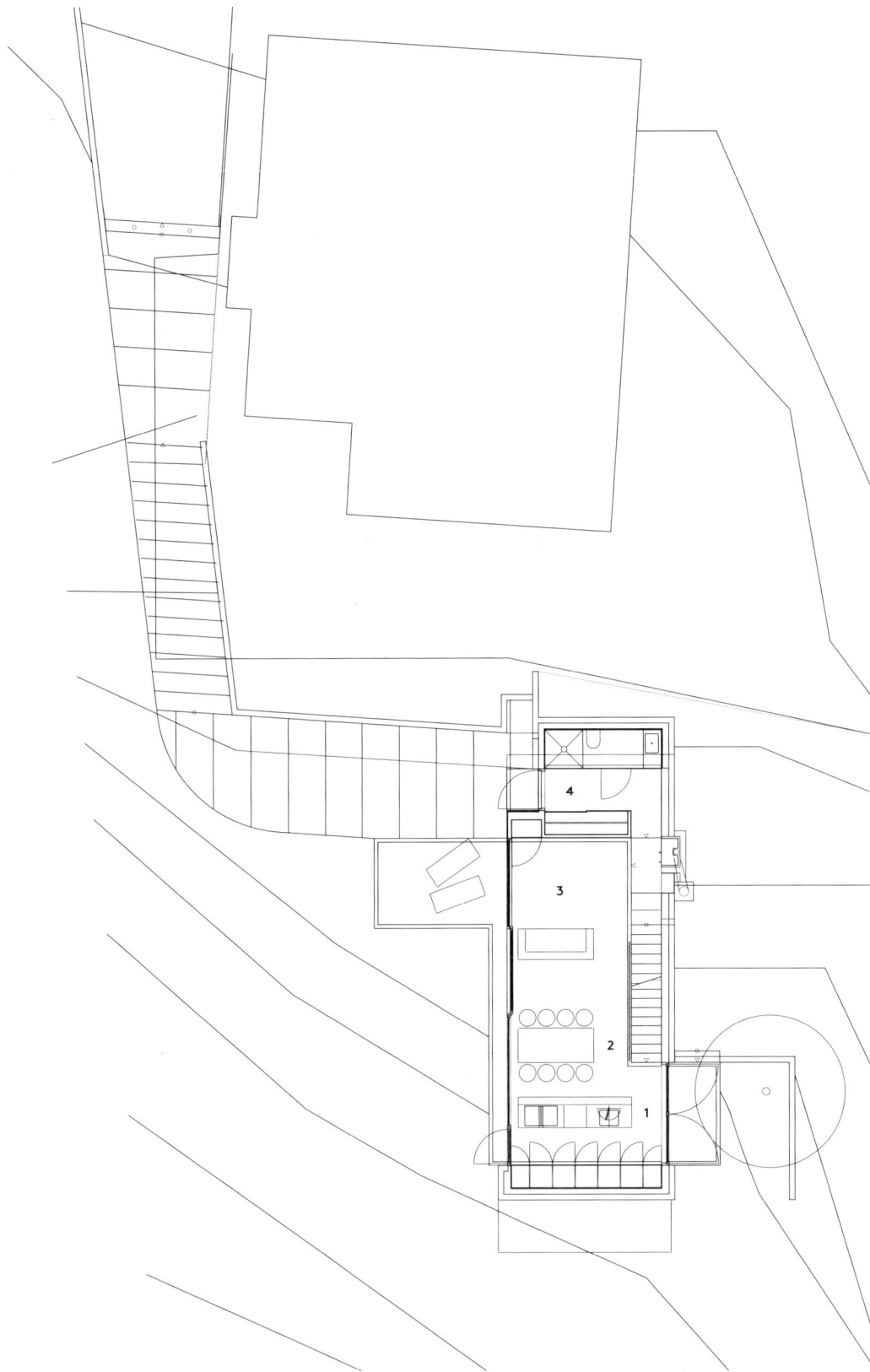

SECOND LEVEL PLAN

0   10 FT

1. Kitchen

2. Dining room

3. Living room

4. Bathroom

ENEBOLIG SØMME

MAISON BAMBOU
BESSANCOURT, FRANCE

Karawitz, 2009

Achieving Passivhaus certification isn't easy, and that's the point. The International Passivhaus Association requires architects wishing to certify their designs to meet stringent criteria for heating, cooling, energy consumption, insulation, and comfort—and essentially guarantee that a structure will sip energy rather than gulp it.

Maison Bambou is 1,722 square feet and France's first certified Passivhaus, completed in 2009 in Bessancourt, northwest of Paris. It was designed by the Paris-based firm Karawitz, founded in 2006 by architects Milena Karanesheva and Mischa Witzmann, who also happened to be the clients for this project. "We built it for us," says Karanesheva, with pride, and the "us" in this case holds a direct and uncompromising design philosophy, which follows the spare quote by the architect Roland Rainer, "I do not want the new, but the just."

What is just about Maison Bambou? Its contextuality—a saltbox farmhouse, built in a region dominated by farmhouses, that's been "dressed in bamboo," according to the design team. The house has two looks, open and closed, so when Karanesheva and Witzmann say "dressed," they literally mean enveloped by what they call a second skin of bamboo. Over time, the untreated skin will turn gray, bringing the house in alignment with older barns in the area. A justifiable addition to the neighborhood.

Beyond embracing the local vernacular of Bessancourt, Karanesheva and Witzmann have equipped this house to perform at high levels of energy efficiency. Maison Bambou includes a solar array on the roof, which generates enough power to reduce its energy consumption to an impressive eleven kilowatt hours of energy per square meter (below the Passivhaus requirement of fifteen). To maximize the sun's warmth in winter, the living spaces face south (and the utilities and service spaces face north), and the interior spaces are optimally ventilated to balance out the sun's rays in summer. This last part is where the bamboo comes in—the culms are kept whole, and not sliced along the frontal plane, to form slats on enormous shutters. In the closed position—when the house is "dressed" with its second skin—the shutters act as light baffles that help the building (and its inhabitants) breathe. "Bamboo is used on the facades for its light and transparent appearance, from outside and inside, as well as [for its] sun protection, and the simplicity of its fixing to the structure," says Karanesheva. The bamboo arrived as rolled mats, which were affixed and rolled down, she says, adding that "it was much easier compared to common wood cladding, [attached] one nail at a time."

Bessancourt is not the first place one would look for bamboo, but after seeing how well it performs in this region, it's now one of the first places architecture media have gone to tout the success of the Passivhaus concept, which originated in Germany and Austria.

"We regarded the local climate first on an empirical level through analysis of orientation, shading, and the local surroundings. Then with the more scientific help of the Passive House Planning Package, which takes into account all the local climate figures to calculate thermal efficiency," says Karanesheva, citing the modeling software that's an industry standard used by both architects and builders.

However, there was no software to help Karanesheva and Witzmann make decisions as their own client. "It was easy and hard," they report. "We made all the basic design decisions very rapidly and without much discussion." But the architects cited basic things that vex most homeowners, like too little storage space. How did two architects and homeowners solve the challenges they designed themselves? They started over. "We did this better on our second house for ourselves, where we live now."

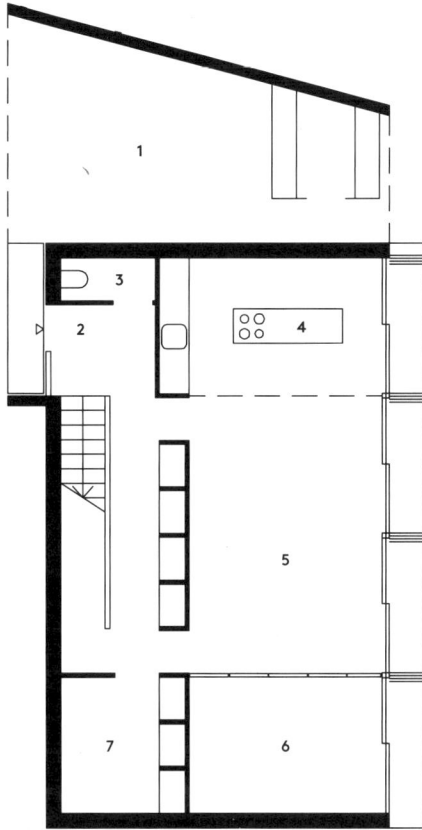

FIRST FLOOR PLAN

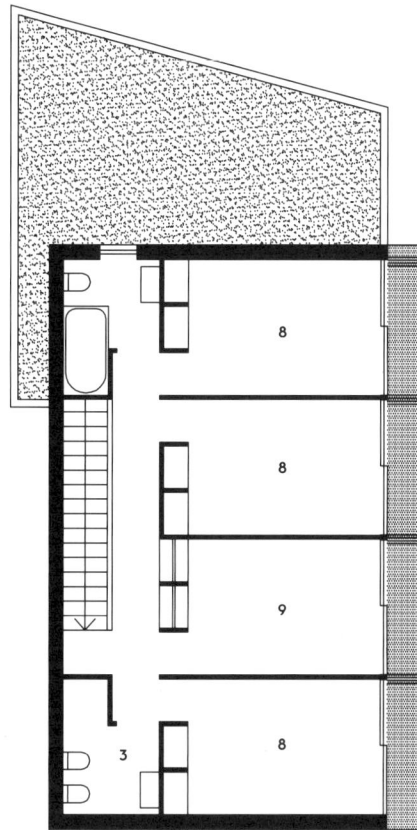

SECOND FLOOR PLAN

0   10 FT

1. Carport

2. Entrance

3. Bathroom

4. Kitchen

5. Living room

6. Music room

7. Technical room

8. Bedroom

9. Library

CASA 01
CRICÚMA, BRAZIL

ES Arquitectura, 2017

In the first half of the twentieth century, Brazil was considered a ripe opportunity for European and American modernists to design *ex novo*, as well as adjacent to (and apart from) the scores of colonial, baroque, and neoclassical icons of São Paulo, Rio de Janeiro, Recife, and Salvador. One of the stylistic achievements of modern architecture was Brasília, designed by Oscar Niemeyer, Lúcio Costa, and Joaquim Cardozo, and it is the ultimate capital city: monumental, spare, and triumphant. Brasília is a raft of rational planning in the Brazilian highlands completed in 1960, which symbolizes an existential state of perfect modernity as a home for the state itself.

To find this project in Cricúma, about five hundred miles south of São Paulo, then makes sense. São Paulo is where Le Corbusier spent time in 1929, joyriding in a prop plane piloted by Antoine de Saint-Exupéry and designing linear megastructures for the fifth largest country in the world. Casa 01 picks up where the International Style left off, hitting all of its "five points" but with several upgrades to keep pace with sustainability standards of the twenty-first century. Some of those upgrades are subtle, like the exposed concrete that has been coated with titanium dioxide, which encourages photocatalysis to remove nitrogen oxides in the air (otherwise known as smog-eating paint). Other upgrades are more obvious, like a gray-water system and photovoltaic panels, a green roof that complements the Corbusian notion of a garden in the sky, and the long, industrial windows that promote cross-ventilation while also invoking Villa Savoye, Villa La Roche, and other Le Corbusier commissions from the 1920s.

Bamboo is another highly visible strategy to broadcast Casa 01's green bona fides. For ES Arquitectura's three principal architects, Diego Espírito Santo, Rodrigo Estrella, and Vânia Marroni Burigo, it was the only solution, given the preponderance of bamboo in Brazil. Specifically, Casa 01 employs Moso (*Phyllostachys edulis*), an Asian species imported by Japanese immigrants in the 1910s and 1920s, characterized by its long culms, approximately sixty-five feet tall. "We are talking about a highly resistant fiber with enormous growth and renewal power that, depending on the species, adapts perfectly in different weather conditions, in snowy areas and in arid climates," says Santo, the project's lead architect, speaking of Moso.

It is lightweight and flexible, has high carbon-sequestration power due to its rapid growth, and can be used either as biomass or in its natural state."

Santo incorporated bamboo into nearly every living space—as the posts and beams of the outdoor dining pergola, as framing elements that make the living room appear to be a series of apertures, as doorjambs and doors, as cladding for accent walls, and as decking. It's a material the firm would like to see more of across architectural production, regardless of the sector.

"Bamboo is undoubtedly and will increasingly be one of the major solutions in combating the mitigation of climate emergencies," says Santo, who advocates swapping out as much masonry, plastic, and metal as possible on job sites, including pipes. "In addition to the direct cost benefits, bamboo has logistical benefits, with shorter assembly times, lighter equipment required, and smaller volumes of workers to handle it." While Casa 01 represents what Santo calls the "concept of sustainability," it goes beyond the conceptual to deliver something uniquely green in response to the client's request for "an icon that represents something innovative."

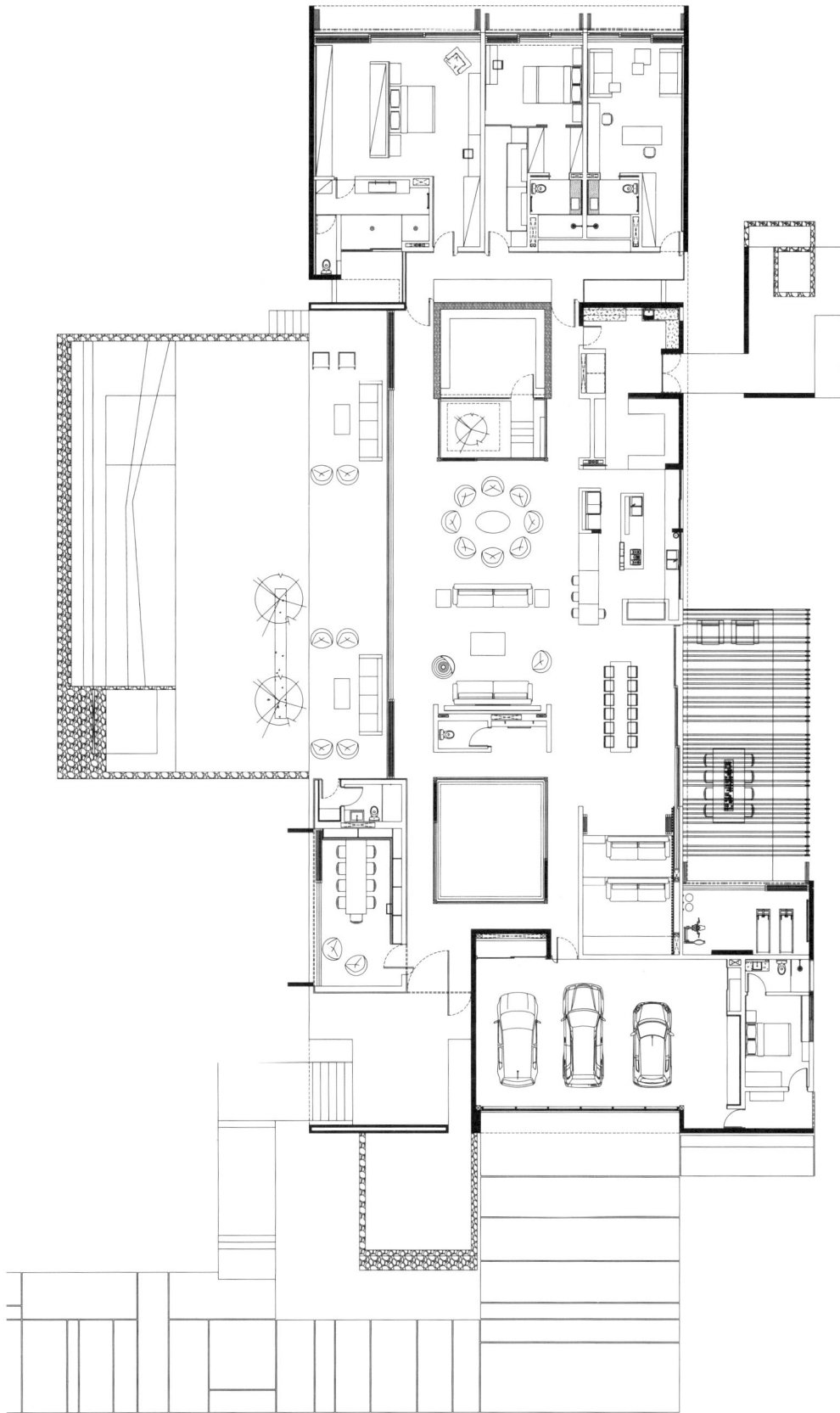

GROUND FLOOR PLAN

0   10 FT

CASA BAMBU
PIPA BEACH, BRAZIL

Vilela Flórez, 2017

Pipa Beach is about as far east as you can go in Brazil—a former fishing village cosseted by cliffs to the north and sandy flats to the south. Since Pipa Beach's state of Rio Grande do Norte wisely established an ecological zone to the west, its growth as a resort destination has been somewhat tempered, making it one of the more exclusive oceanside enclaves, uphill and inland from the crowds.

Architects Mariana Vilela and Daniel Fernández Flórez set out to design a vacation home for a septuagenarian couple (Flórez's parents), who wanted a home to host their adult children and their families, with one caveat: it had to be completed in ten months. Less than a year later, they delivered Casa Bambu, which consists of three nearly identical and individually owned condominium units oriented to pull the prevailing southerly breezes across the garden and the pool and through to the interior living spaces. Each unit contains a bathroom and utility space and one bedroom that opens out to a shared patio and outdoor kitchen.

It's an uncomplicated indoor-outdoor living arrangement, with an emphasis on family time and communal meals. From a design perspective, what elevates the house is the architects' use of bamboo as cladding in a visually striking herringbone pattern—with a twist. The bamboo cladding doubles as a baffle for light and a natural ventilation system for air, encouraging the cross-breezes that keep sleeping conditions temperate. There are other practical reasons for using bamboo poles that have been cut lengthwise and used as cladding—they are easy to remove, section by section, to repair or replace. When used as cladding, bamboo is its own modular maintenance solution.

"We found it interesting—the aesthetic dialogue between the diagonal effect of the bamboo in a herringbone pattern and the vertical rhythms of the columns," say Vilela and Flórez. They point out that the construction of the facade is also a way to conceal the systems within the walls—notably the drainpipes running from roof to ground.

Vilela and Flórez established their firm in 2014, after working at Herzog and de Meuron in Basel, Switzerland. Their first project together was their own seaside studio in Tibau do Sul, about five miles north of Pipa Beach. They started with very little capital and few connections in the area, but they were committed to finding a new way of working that focused on regionally sourced materials. "When we left Herzog and de Meuron, we had to rethink our design process, so we tried to analyze the local elements and [find] constructive solutions. We wanted to revisit them and improve them by pushing boundaries."

Thanks to its adaptive qualities, bamboo is a good medium to push those boundaries. They selected Fish Pole Bamboo (*Phyllostachys aurea*) from São Paulo. Fish Pole Bamboo, which also is one of the most common species grown in the United States (particularly along the East Coast from Connecticut to Florida), has a few natural color variations—true gold, green cane with gold stripes, and gold cane with green stripes. It is not an adequate structural bamboo, report Vilela and Flórez, but it is often used for ornamental reasons, as demonstrated at Casa Bambu. In its natural state, this species can be found growing in side yards and back yards across the southeastern United States. Its lush foliage can

double as a screen to the street or neighbors.

After slicing the poles lengthwise to place in Casa Bambu's rectilinear frame, Vilela and Flórez added polyurethane foam to the pole ends to protect the exposed fibers from water. They also treated the ten-foot pole lengths with two kinds of varnish to protect them, after lightly sanding the surface to remove the natural waxy skin that rejects varnish.

All for good reason: the Caatinga ecoregion is known for its dry winters and wet summers, with very little variation in between. In fact, it's South America's largest tropical dry-forest area. It also hosts a vulnerable but diverse ecosystem that's consistently under threat from climate change in the form of severe droughts, which have set records in Brazil during the last decade.

Climate pressures on agriculture have also been exacerbated by demographic pressures. Natal, the largest city near Pipa Beach, perched on the eastern edge of Caatinga, has doubled its population in the last thirty years. All of those people need food, and as Pipa Beach's growing popularity has underscored, some of them would like to spend a weekend at the beach once in a while too.

Still, there are vestiges of the old way of doing things—traditional building techniques are still desirable, even if the area is awash in new money and new tourists. "We designed these elements with local workers, in order to provide a fresh approach and reinterpret their traditional values in a contemporary and sustainable way," Vilela and Flórez say. "And we think that Casa Bambu fulfills this philosophy."

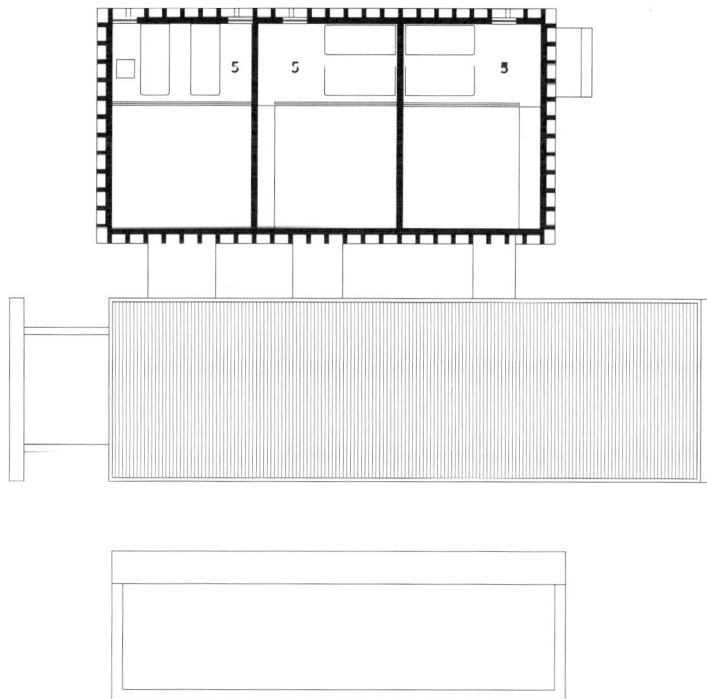

MEZZANINE FLOOR PLAN

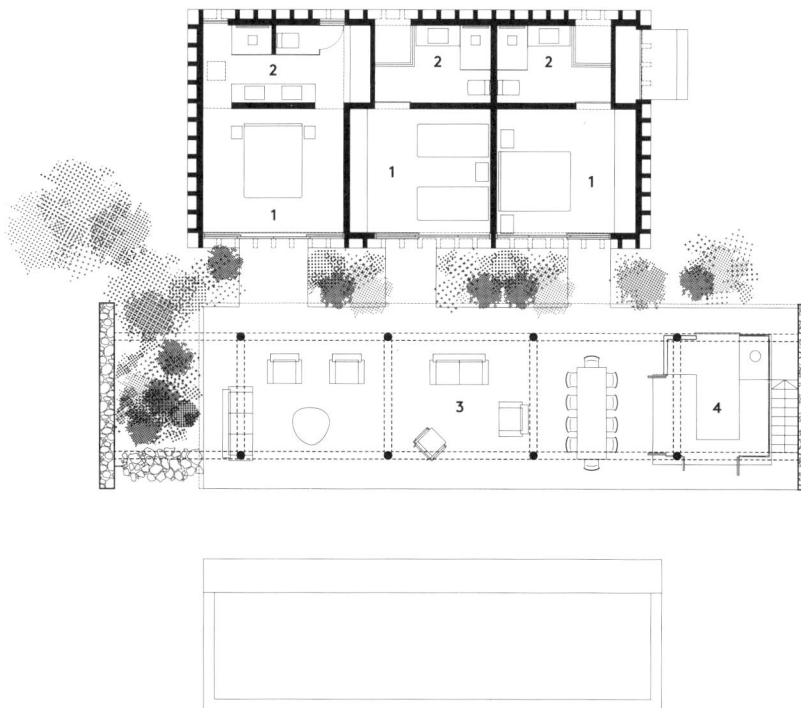

GROUND FLOOR PLAN

0   10FT

1.   Bedrooms

2.   Bathrooms

3.   Open living spaces

4.   Kitchen

5.   Mezzanine

CASA BAMBU

CASA BAMBU

CASA DON JUAN
MANABÍ, ECUADOR

Emilio López Arquitecto, 2018

Most of Emilio López Herrera's half-dozen or so residential commissions have a few things in common, beyond his occasional use of bamboo that is characteristic of his particular brand of contextual modernism. One thing stands out though: his obsession with apertures. Enormous windows consistently maximize natural light in his spare, but texturally rich, interiors. In the case of his Casa Don Juan, in Manabí, Ecuador's westernmost province, he transforms the house into something akin to the trapezoidal prism of an early single-lens reflex camera.

In plan, the house reveals a gentle catenary swoop and takes something from Eero Saarinen and Oscar Niemeyer. Herrera describes his Manabí project as a funnel. It's oriented west–east to capture both ocean and forest views and optimized to catch the breezes his client wanted to experience during her stay there during weekends away from her university professorship in Quito. "The client sought, above all, that the house has an important view toward the sea. But in the different interviews we had, I understood that, what she wanted was an important link with the environment," says Herrera.

The low-slung roofline shelters the home's kitchen and dining area at the center of the house. The apertures (or funnel ends, as Herrera sees them) admit salty air on one side and the sweet musk of palo santo trees on the other into two double-height spaces that include sleeping and lounging areas on the second floor. This arrangement of spaces is an important way to passively cool the house. It also suggests sitting and sipping aguardiente sours like a modern-day Don Juan—but why the name Don Juan? It's not about Mozart's muse, nor is it about the Seducer of Seville, Don Giovanni. It's simply the name of the nearest town (which, itself, is probably named for the Spanish libertine, although this is unconfirmed).

The interior of the home exudes warmth, due in large part to floor-to-ceiling Pau Amarillo, a wood otherwise known as yellowheart, and feels as rustic as a high plains cabin or as obsessively structural as a Japanese moongaze cottage. Herrera's use of bamboo is less obvious, contained within composite panels hung on the exterior and plastered over to signal the project's modern bona fides. "Don Juan House uses materials from the area in a simple and low-cost construction system, which, for me, means consistency in design," says Herrera. "The bamboo in this project allows us to achieve an internal warmth at a very adequate cost. But, at the same time, this same material, being plastered with cement mortar and mesh outside, gives protection to the house against moisture and external conditions."

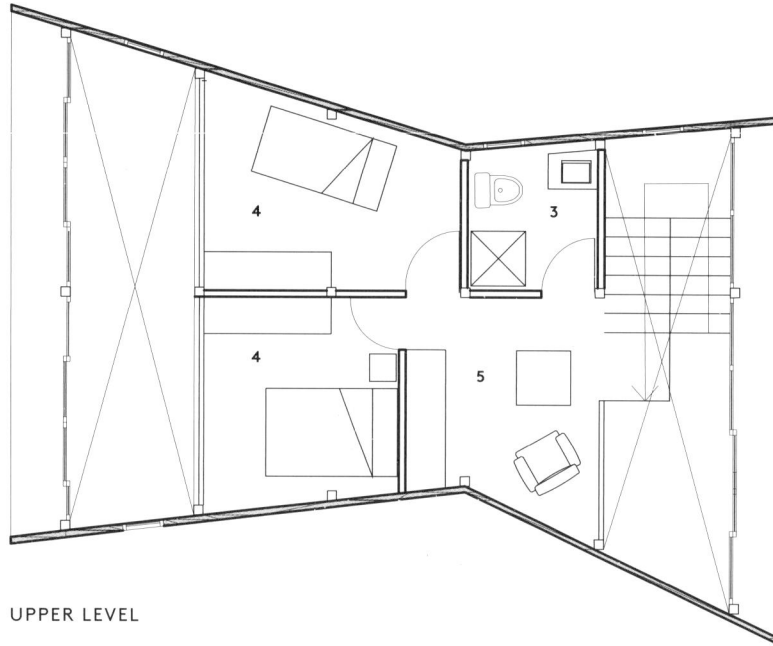

UPPER LEVEL

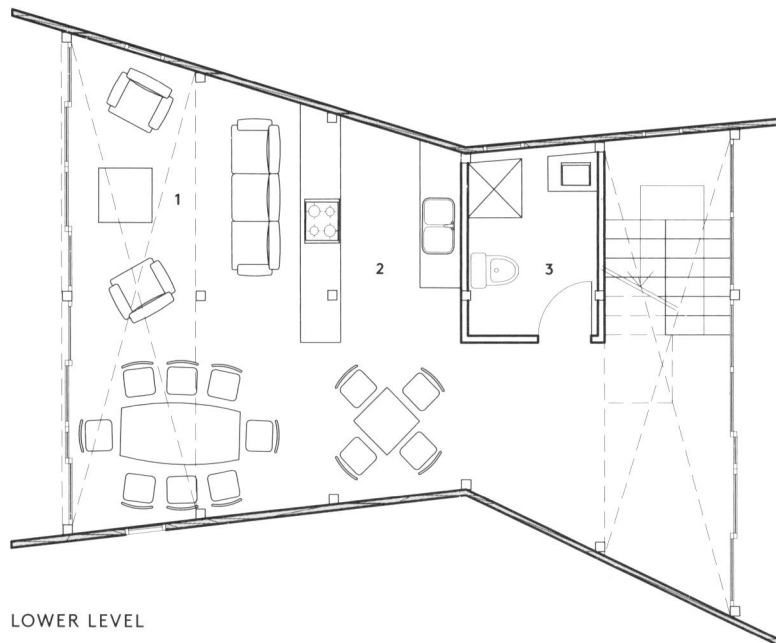

LOWER LEVEL

0   10FT

1. Living room
2. Kitchen
3. Bathroom
4. Bedroom
5. Study

GRASS HOUSE
WASHINGTON, DC

bld.us, 2018

When the architect is the client on a project, the only limit is budget—and even that can be more of a suggestion than a boundary. In the case of Grass House, in Washington, DC, architects Andrew Linn and Jack Becker have delivered what they call a "case study, mock-up, and workspace" that they can use to illustrate the potential of bamboo products. By all outward appearances, though, its modest scale and conventional accoutrements do not suggest a radical experiment but rather something more familiar, like a cottage, or, if you're standing on axis with the entrance, a cozy dacha. At a cost of $200,000, this seven-hundred-gross-square-foot project is relatively modest in budget too, without wasting a single opportunity to experiment. Surrounding the house is a three-hundred-square-foot rock garden and a five-hundred-square-foot flowering rain garden, aiding drainage and creating a peaceful glade in one of the densest urban regions in the country.

Becker and Linn charred the outside of the house to seal the wood and made the inside a showcase of natural materials, like ash, cork, oak, and, notably, bamboo in the form of dual-panel wall systems manufactured by BamCore (and filled with sheep's wool for insulation). The wall system is a sandwich of laminated veneer bamboo slices, compressed to a thickness of one-quarter inch, further wrapped with Douglas fir veneers, making the whole panel about one-and-one-quarter inch thick. Thermal bridging, or the degree to which heat is conveyed through a wall and a structure loses energy, is largely mitigated by the wall's bamboo system. Across the different framing sizes offered by the manufacturer, the R-value is consistently about 25 to 26 percent higher than conventional walls.

Becker and Linn's use of this wall system is only half the story. The visual centerpiece inside is a vertical willow-reed partition that extends from the basement up through the first floor and into the second. While willow reeds at this small scale are usually soaked in order to make them pliable, and woven into baskets, Becker and Linn left them rigid to divide circulation space from living space (and wove them only a few times through vertical standards in a nod to the craftways they both appreciate). The effect is elemental in appearance and rugged to the touch but also deceptively delicate looking: the twiggy and sinuous willow sticks are, by Becker and Linn's estimation, far stronger than drywall.

Becker, who grew up just beyond the city's upper northwest boundary, in suburban Maryland, is familiar with the city's carriage houses, which were once a defining and pervasive feature of everyday life and now incredibly rare. Becker and Linn took the carriage house as the starting point, swapped wood clapboards for bamboo, and adapted the building type.

The alleys where you're likely to find carriage houses in the Mid-Atlantic region have continued to play an important role in urban life. Alleys are still where you're likely to bring your trash and recycling, and park your car, but they're also frequently used cut-throughs and, occasionally, passages to inter-block oases like Roxborough Pocket Park in Philadelphia or Scuffletown Park in Richmond, Virginia. In Washington, DC, carriage house renovations have driven millions of dollars of redevelopment in recent years for both commercial and residential clients, almost always in the spirit of their original appearance. Notably, these renovations have been important counterpoints the metal-clad,

six- and seven-story apartment buildings that have come to define gentrification in the nation's capital. To that end, Anacostia's rich urban fabric is defined by its nineteenth- and early-twentieth century homes, carriage houses, and out-buildings, and Anacostia is, in many respects, a microcosm of the building stock and heritage of the entire mid-Atlantic.

"It's about relating to the historic context of Anacostia without being historicist," says Andrew Linn. "In Anacostia, there's the desire, but not the budget, to build [in] such a sustainable way. In the upper northwest neighborhoods, by contrast, there's the budget, but not the desire. So, we are trying to bridge an economic gap in DC."

The Grass House is remarkable as a contribution to Anacostia, a historic commercial and residential neighborhood of the city that's a living pattern book for architectural styles spanning a century. Frederick Douglass's home and writing retreat sit a stone's throw from Becker and Linn's Grass House, and both properties sit in the geographic middle of the Anacostia Historic District. It's a challenging place, though, with good bones, a tight-knit community, and the highest percentage of native Washingtonians in the city, but it also has a high crime rate and an unemployment rate that's routinely three to four times the national average.

Still, Linn and Becker have committed to their adopted neighborhood, its contrasts as well as its challenges. The Grass House might be the start of Anacostia's next chapter, or it might be an incubator for the firm's next big idea. Either way, it's an architectural laboratory that will be an anchor for its alley, and street, for years to come.

SECTION

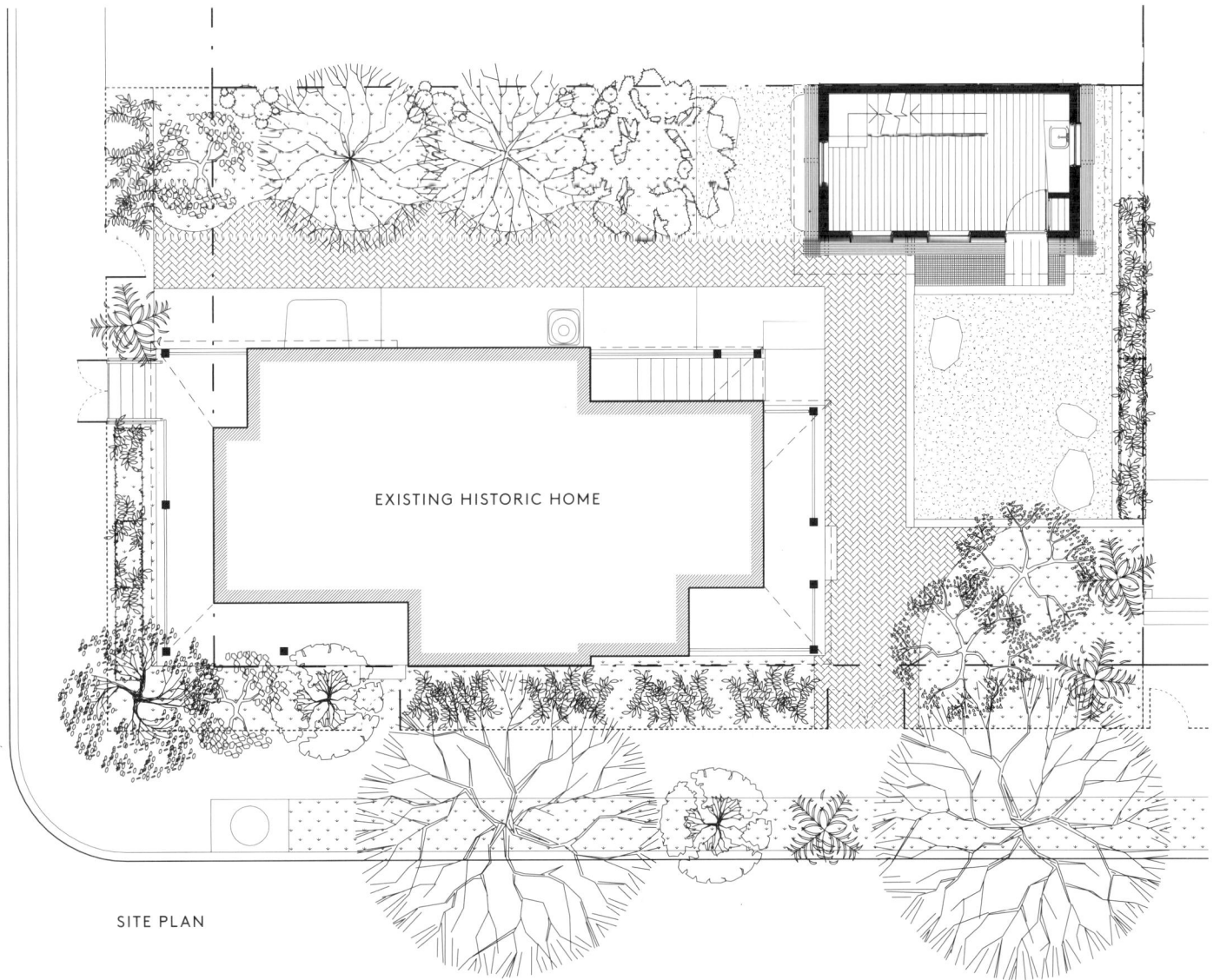

EXISTING HISTORIC HOME

SITE PLAN

0   10 FT

ONE JACKSON SQUARE
NEW YORK, NEW YORK

Kohn Pedersen Fox, 2011

Tiny Jackson Square Park in New York can be easily overlooked amid the din of the daily bustle. At a point where five streets and four neighborhoods intersect, the triangular plot was in the eighteenth and nineteenth centuries the site of rallies and even earlier marked the crook of a vital Lenape artery.

One Jackson Square, a thirty-unit condominium, doesn't preside over its eponymous park so much as it sidles up to it with ribbon windows that form transverse waves, providing both a sense of movement and a backdrop to the pedestrian life of the street. There's a disruption in the waves, though, in the form of the building's entry and lobby that feels far less aqueous than the facade.

The lobby is clad in sixty-five panels each composed of 185 bamboo strips fabricated by SITU Studio, which specializes in making seemingly impossible architectural elements and furniture at its Brooklyn Navy Yard production facility. If these panels make the space remarkable, one's procession through it makes the lobby feel inescapable. Bits of stone embedded in the terrazzo floor evoke a riverbed, and silver leaf in the ceiling enhances the warm glow of the panels.

"Antelope Canyon in Arizona resonated with me," says Kohn Pedersen Fox's (KPF) Trent Tesch, "and we were definitely trying to achieve the feeling of a real place, rather than just a lobby."

Tesch, who describes the plan of the building as "California-shaped," reports that the canyon parti derives from site constraints, as One Jackson Square sits atop three subway lines, which skirt the Greenwich Avenue side of the narrow plot. That meant the elevator shafts couldn't be dug near the entrance and had to be placed toward the rear of the site, necessitating a long walk across California, as it were, for comers and goers.

"We struggled because of the subway below, so the elevators had to be pushed way to the back of the lobby. That was the inspiration for the imagery of the canyon," says Tesch. "We stuck with the idea of erosion and took that language into the lobby, and so we ended up achieving something almost psychedelic and dream-like."

Smith & Fong Plyboo manufactured the three-and-a-quarter-inch-thick, three-ply sheets that, in section, show two thin layers sandwiching a thick crosscut layer, created in much the same heat-pressed way as conventional plywood. KPF tested several materials to achieve the look and feel of a natural canyon, including various woods, but landed on bamboo for its versatility and durability. KPF shipped its three-dimensional models to Basar Girit, a founding partner at SITU, who converted the dimensions into individual panels that could be fabricated and nested together. As seamless as the panels appear, there is a hand-laid quality to them at the vertical seams, creating syncopated markers that pull people through the lobby whether they're coming or going: no lingering or waiting, only moving. "It was an interesting problem," says Tesch. "Where do you start a lobby, and where do you stop a lobby? So, instead of ending it, we decided to let the lobby greet you at the street, rather than making you wait until you get inside."

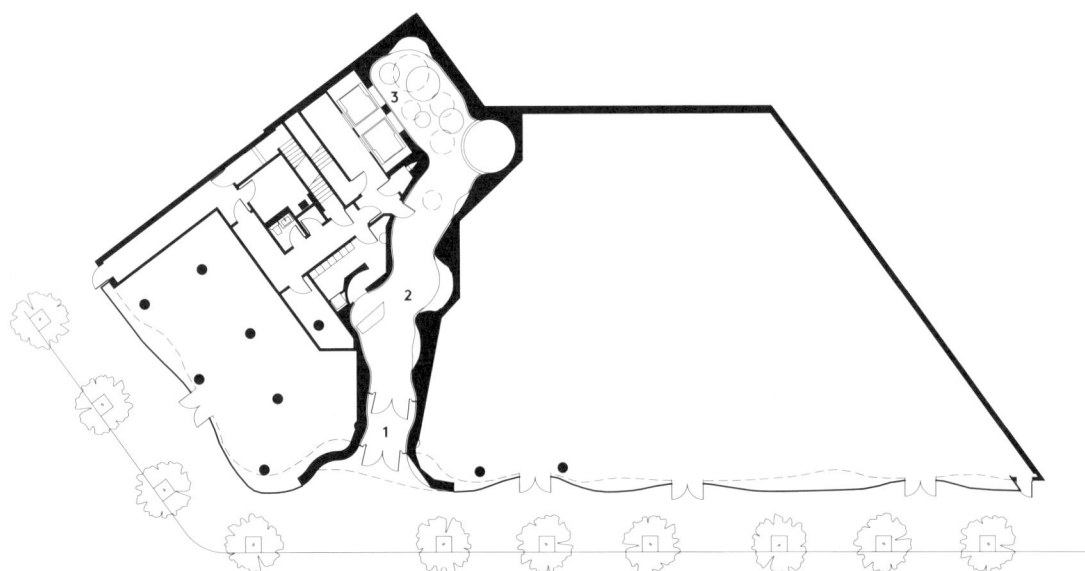

1. Entrance
2. Lobby
3. Elevator lobby

GROUND FLOOR PLAN

0   10 FT

ONE JACKSON SQUARE

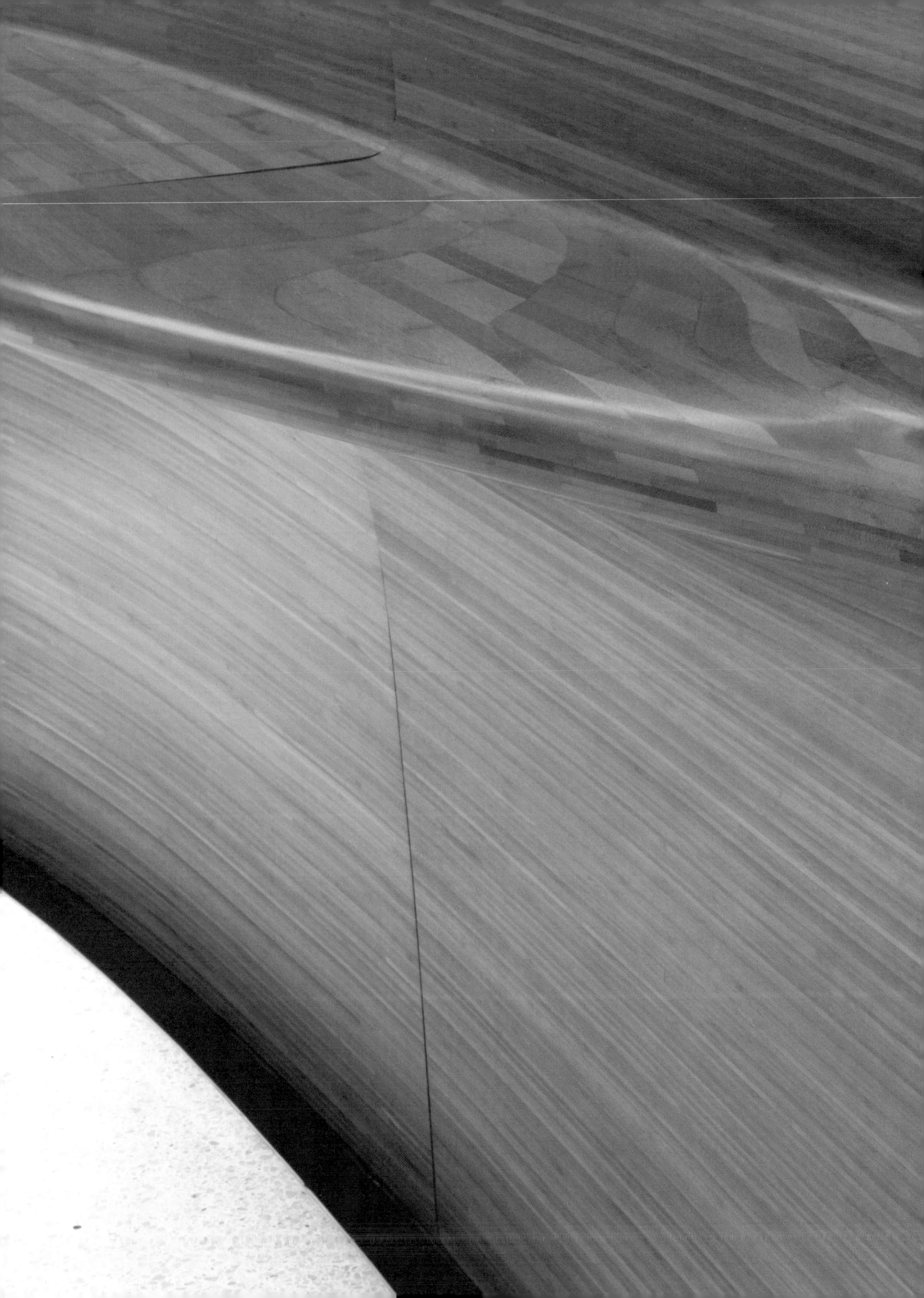

PAKALANA SANCTUARY
KAMUELA, HAWAII

Bamboo Living, 2012

The island of Hawaii is the largest in the archipelago that bears its name, and it's the most rugged—appealing to more adventurous vacationers and offering residents a spectrum of climate zones, from snowy peaks to rocky beaches. The island's five major shield volcanoes, so called for their low rise resembling a shield on the ground, cover every square mile of the island. Four of these shield-volcano zones converge at the northwest corner of Hawaii and funnel into a large cove fronted by Hāpuna Beach State Recreation Area, which features a white sand beach routinely ranked among the best in the world.

Pakalana Sanctuary, a residential resort designed by David Sands, founder and principal of Bamboo Living, sits two miles south of Hāpuna Beach. Its asymmetrical cour d'honneur is flanked by two-story wings with low-slung roofs and a post-and-beam construction that creates a visual rhythm laterally across and into the recesses of the upper-level walkways. It's a familiar way of organizing space for a multiunit apartment building or even a motel to create an inward-facing enclave from the road, and usually with a swimming pool at the center. At Pakalana, however, it's a form that's nearly unrecognizable, eclipsed by a surfeit of bamboo—as structure, cladding, and fittings. Pakalana uses *Bambusa stenostachya*, native to the Quảng Ngãi Province of central Vietnam, which is hearty enough and thick enough to be used as erosion control along rivers and appropriate for Hawaii, which has a five- to six-month wet season.

Sands works almost exclusively in bamboo at his firm, which he cofounded with Jeffree Trudeau in 1995. Bamboo Living designs and sells a range of modular, prefabricated models that clients can customize. Bamboo Living also controls its own supply chain, ensuring that the bamboo it sources, prepares, ships to its factory, and reassembles on site is sustainable and contributes to what Sands calls an "organic, breathing home."

Pakalana combines elements of the models Sands and his team developed over time, which are adjusted to accommodate the two flood zones that converge on the site. County code demands for outdoor circulation met by a series of connected walkways and the adjacencies of a six-room resort that must balance privacy and convenience. Above all else, the resort had to live up to the promise that words like *luxury* and *sanctuary* imply, so this new composition of independent prototypes Sands typically uses for private homes had to seem more than an international design vision. It had to seem transcendent.

"There's a peacefulness to being inside spaces conceived and built of bamboo. It has to do with the material's quality itself but also the handcrafted nature of it," says Sands, who has been working with bamboo for thirty years. He estimates that each bamboo project saves about ten to twelve acres of trees that would otherwise become lumber for conventional buildings. Sands would like to scale-up his bamboo cultivation and sourcing operation through Bamboo Living, producing raw and treated culms in the Philippines and, ideally, Florida. "We're committed to developing its potential," he says. "Building houses out of bamboo poles is beautiful, but it's not yet at a scale to impact the climate positively, which is obviously what we need to do."

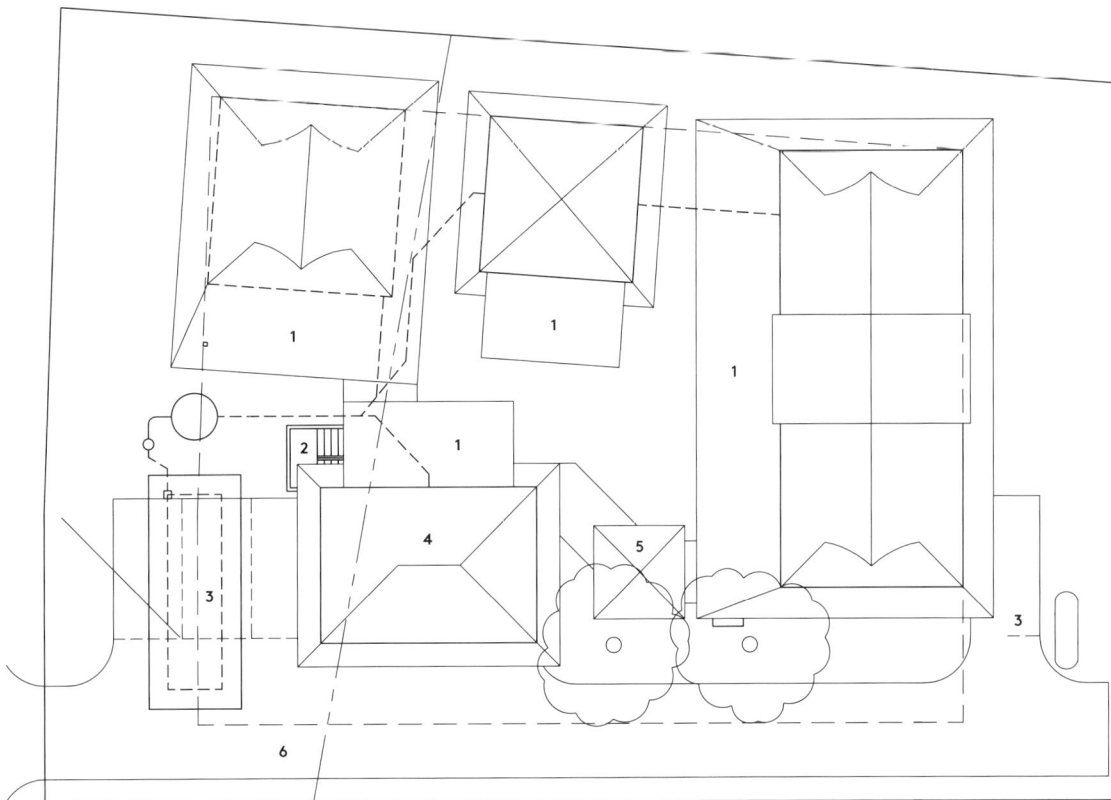

SITE PLAN

0   10 FT

1. Covered porch
2. Stairs
3. Parking stalls
4. Carport
5. BBQ area
6. Driveway

Acknowledgments

This is my first book with Princeton Architectural Press, and I'm grateful to my colleagues there including Michelle Meier, Parker Menzimer, Stephanie Holstein, Joe Weston, Jessica Tackett, Wes Seeley, Abby Bussel, Linda Lee, Paul Wagner, Paula Baver, Kristen Hewitt, the sales team, and the publisher, Lynn Grady. Thank you all for your commitment to this project. I am also indebted to Jan Hartman for being this book's first champion and editor. Without her tenacity and guidance, this project wouldn't have happened. I am also grateful to the architects and designers I interviewed for their time and candor over the course of many months. I especially want to acknowledge my first interview subjects, Jack Becker and Andrew Linn, cofounders of bld. us, as well as Luc Boeraeve, president of the American Bamboo Society, whose input at critical times proved helpful and inspiring. I am also grateful to William Morgan for his support throughout my research for this book, not to mention countless other writing projects during two decades of friendship. Finally, I must thank my wife and partner, Pascale Vonier, for her patience, support, enthusiasm, and critical eye. She has made this a better book than I could have ever made on my own.